SUPERPORTRAITS

Superportraits
Caricatures and Recognition

Gillian Rhodes
University of Western Australia

Psychology Press
An imprint of Erlbaum (UK) Taylor & Francis

Psychology Press, Publishers
27 Church Road
Hove
East Sussex, BN3 2FA
UK

British Library Cataloguing in Publication Data

A catalogue record for this book is available from the British Library

    ISBN 0-86377-398-2

Printed and bound in the UK by TJ Press, Padstow, Cornwall

Contents

Acknowledgements

In 1984, my PhD advisor Roger Shepard introduced me to Susan Brennan, who had developed a computer Caricature Generator at the MIT Media Lab, and Susan Carey, an expert in the study of face recognition. Meeting the two Susans stimulated the interest in caricatures that led to this book and I thank them for the intellectual excitement and warmth of their friendship. I am also grateful to Mike Corballis and Roger Shepard for fostering my early interests in face recognition and mental representation.

I began writing this book while on sabbatical leave from the University of Canterbury, and I thank my hosts Susan Carey, at the Massachusetts Institute of Technology, Marjorie Taylor at the University of Oregon at Eugene, and Darwin Muir at Queen's University for their hospitality, as well as my own institution for granting me leave.

I also thank the many collaborators, students, and research assistants who have contributed to some of the studies discussed in Chapters 1, 6, and 7. Special thanks are due to Susan Carey, Susan Brennan, Tanya Tremewan, Mark Tremewan, Ian McLean, Susan Brake, Shirley Tan, and Graham Byatt. This work has been supported by the University Grants Committee of New Zealand, the Social Science Research Committee of New Zealand, the Foundation for Research, Science and Technology, the New Zealand Lotteries Board, and the Psychology Departments of Stanford University, Otago University and

Canterbury University. I thank them all for their generous support.

I am also grateful to colleagues and reviewers who commented on earlier drafts or parts of the manuscript: Mike Corballis, William Hayward, Fiona Proffitt, Ken Strongman, Jack Copeland, Nancy Etcoff, Ian Jamieson, Geoffrey White, Hadyn Ellis, and an anonymous reviewer. Finally, I thank Tanya Tremewan for preparing the indices, and Rohays Perry and the staff at Psychology Press for all their efforts.

CHAPTER ONE

Introduction

... an object that is novel and yet similar to an already significant object may especially warrant our close attention. We need to know how far something can depart from its usual or expected form and still have the consequences that we have found to follow from its "natural kind". In doing so, we also come closer to an understanding of the critical features of a stimulus that elicits a resonant response within us and, thus, closer to an understanding of ourselves.

Shepard (1990) p.202

THE CHALLENGE OF CARICATURES

As Nixon's popularity plummeted during Watergate, his nose and jowls grew to impossible proportions in published caricatures. Yet the caricatures remained instantly recognisable. In some cases caricatures are even *superportraits*, with the paradoxical quality of being more like the face than the face itself. As one viewer of a television programme featuring caricatured puppets exclaimed, "Hell the one of Bill Cosby looks more like Bill Cosby than Bill Cosby does!".

The power of caricatures sets a challenge for those of us who are interested in how recognition works. How can such obviously distorted images be more recognisable than undistorted images? Indeed, how can

1

they be recognised at all? Do caricatures exploit some special property of a face recognition system, or are they effective for a variety of objects, capitalising on some more fundamental preference for exaggeration? These are the kinds of questions that I will address in this book. Along the way I will also explore the role of exaggeration in art and nature, looking for clues about the kind of mental representations and recognition processes from which caricatures might derive their power.

RECOGNITION

Before turning the spotlight onto caricatures, let me begin with some background about recognition. The ability to recognise objects by their appearance supports an enormous range of activities. It allows us to find food, to avoid predation, to orient ourselves using landmarks, to recognise people, and to maintain a complex network of social interactions.

Recognition occurs automatically and without conscious effort, but it is no mean feat. In order to recognise what we see, we must convert the complex, but ephemeral, patterns of light energy reaching our eyes into stable, familiar, and meaningful representations. To recognise objects the visual system must solve two problems. The first is caused by the huge variety of appearances that an object can present due to changes in our viewpoint.[1] To recognise an object we must be able to map a potentially infinite set of images onto a single object representation, i.e. we must solve the *object constancy problem.*

The second problem stems from the extreme similarity of objects like faces. Our expertise with faces can blind us to their similarity, but you can get some idea if you look at your old school photographs upside-down, or visit an exotic location where faces are different from those you are used to seeing. Humpty-Dumpty put his finger on the nature of the difficulty, when he complained to Alice that, "You're so exactly like other people ... the two eyes, so (marking their places in the air with his thumb) nose in the middle, mouth under. It's always the same. Now if you had the two eyes on the same side of the nose, for instance—or the mouth at the top—that would be *some* help." (Carroll, 1946). As Humpty-Dumpty observed, faces are difficult to recognise precisely because they have the same basic parts in the same basic arrangement, i.e. because of their homogeneity. Therefore, in order to recognise faces and other objects that share a configuration (birds, dogs, cars, etc.) our visual system must find a way of representing the subtle differences that distinguish such similar objects, i.e. it must solve the *homogeneity problem.*

We know that the visual system has solved these two problems. After all, we routinely recognise familiar objects from different viewpoints and homogeneous objects such as faces. What is less clear is *how* we solve these problems. Let's consider each one in turn.

Solving the object constancy problem

The object constancy problem could potentially be solved in a variety of ways. One way would be to use *view-independent representations* that don't change with changes in viewpoint. Marr (1982) developed this idea, suggesting that the arrangement of an object's parts is described in relation to the main axis of elongation of the object. This axis defines a co-ordinate system, or frame of reference, within which the rest of the parts can be described and located. By describing the object's structure using a co-ordinate system centred on the object itself, the representation does not change with the viewer's perspective.

Another kind of view-independent representation can be obtained by describing the object's structure without reference to any co-ordinate system at all. Biederman (1987, 1990) developed this idea, proposing that we represent objects using a limited vocabulary of simple 3-D shapes called geons. Geons are created by sweeping a cross-sectional shape, like a circle or square, along an axis, and they can be defined by properties that don't change with the observer's viewpoint, such as the curvature, symmetry, and size of the cross-section, and the curvature of the axis.

In both cases the perceptual representation can be compared with stored representations of the same type, and recognition occurs when a match is found. *Viewpoint-invariant representations* seem to offer an elegant and economical solution to the object constancy problem. They are unaffected by changes in one's viewpoint, and only a single representation must be stored for each object. However, they may be difficult or impossible to derive from images. Marr offered no algorithm that could detect the axis of elongation, and some objects do not even have one (e.g. crumpled newspaper, beach balls). Nor is it clear just how successfully geons can be derived from images. Therefore, the economy of storage and ease of matching offered by viewpoint-invariant representations may come at a high computational price, i.e. they are difficult to compute from images.

An alternative solution to the object constancy problem would be to use *view-specific representations*, such as descriptions in retinal co-ordinates. These are much easier to derive from images than view-invariant representations. However, the matching process is more demanding. Unless an enormous set of viewpoints is stored for every object, some transformation (e.g. mental rotation, Tarr & Pinker, 1989;

alignment, Ullman, 1989) will be needed to map a perceptual representation onto the stored descriptions for each familiar object. The set of stored descriptions for an object might consist of a single representation, such as a commonly seen view or a canonical view that shows the most salient features or parts of the object. Alternatively, it might consist of a small set of viewpoints, such as those experienced most frequently or those that display qualitatively different information about the object (e.g. handle-present and handle-absent views of a cup, Koenderink & Van Doorn, 1979).

The relative merits of view-specific and view-independent representations are currently the subject of intensive debate (Biederman, 1995; Biederman & Gerhardstein, 1993, 1995; Corballis, 1988; Rock & Di Vita, 1987; Takano, 1989; Tarr & Bülthoff, 1995; Tarr, Hayward, Gauthier, & Williams, 1994; Tarr & Pinker, 1989, 1990; Ullman, 1989). In addition to the problem of how view-independent representations can be derived from images, those who favour this solution to the object constancy problem must also explain why the orientation of an object, especially orientation in the picture plane, consistently affects recognition performance (e.g. Jolicoeur, 1985; Rock & Di Vita, 1987; Tarr & Pinker, 1989, 1990). After all, the whole point of viewpoint-independent representations is that they are unaffected by such changes in the image. The debate remains unresolved, although some authors have recently suggested a compromise solution, with both types of representation used, but each under different circumstances (e.g. Corballis, 1988; Jolicoeur, 1990; Tarr & Chawarski, 1993). For example, view-invariant representations may be used when the arrangement of parts in a 2-D object differs on a single dimension, but not when it differs on more than one dimension (Tarr & Pinker, 1990).

There is considerable agreement[2] that objects are represented by their component *parts* and the overall spatial arrangement of those parts (Biederman, 1987; Hoffman & Richards, 1984; Marr, 1982) (see Fig. 1.1). A part-based representation is ideal for basic level recognition (Rosch, Mervis et al., 1976)—chair, car, house, dog, tree, etc.—because basic level objects, especially manufactured ones (Corballis, 1991), differ primarily in their parts (Tversky & Hemenway, 1984) and the spatial arrangement of those parts (Biederman, 1987).

However, such a system will not work for all objects. In particular, it won't work for homogeneous objects like faces that have the same basic components in the same basic arrangement. A part-based analysis can tell us that we're looking at a face, but not whose face it is. To recognise an individual face, something subtler than a parts-analysis is needed, something that capitalises on the subtle variations within the shared configuration that are unique to each face.

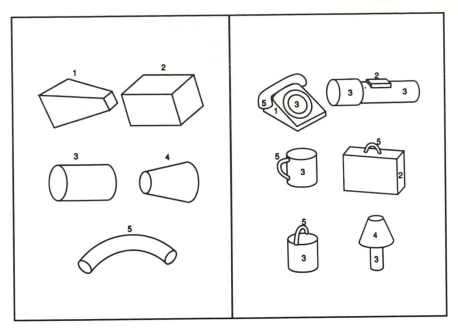

FIG. 1.1. The part-based structure of common objects is illustrated in this figure from Biederman (1990). Examples of geons (volume primitives) are shown on the left. The identity and arrangement (cf. cup and bucket) of geons in some common objects are shown on the right. Reproduced with permission from Biederman (1990).

Solving the homogeneity problem

Diamond and Carey (1986) have sought a solution to the homogeneity problem by considering the constraints imposed by the stimuli themselves. They proposed a continuum of features ranging from relatively isolated to relatively relational features.[3] These features could be anything that is used to distinguish faces. Isolated features can be specified without reference to several parts of the stimulus at once. Examples are the presence and shape of glasses, facial hair, scars, or wrinkles, as well as non-spatial cues like hair colour and texture. Relational features, in contrast, cannot be specified without reference to several parts of the face at once. Examples include ratios of distances and the internal spacing of features.

Although a few faces have distinctive isolated features such as a handlebar moustache or a tell-tale scar, isolated features will not generally suffice for distinguishing the hundreds or even thousands of faces that we can each recognise. Instead, Diamond and Carey suggested that relational features are crucial for face recognition. Moreover, they conjectured that reliance on relational features makes face recognition unusually vulnerable to inversion. Turning faces upside-down disrupts recognition much more than turning other mono-oriented objects upside-down, with accuracy dropping 20–30% for faces compared with 0–10% for other objects (Carey & Diamond, 1994; Diamond & Carey, 1986; Rhodes et al., 1993; Valentine, 1988; Yin, 1969, 1970). Recognition of complex stimuli like landscapes that do not share a configuration is not especially disrupted by inversion, so that a large inversion decrement seems to be a feature of homogeneous objects.

This proposed link between reliance on relational features and large inversion decrements has been confirmed recently. Changes to relational features (e.g. the spacing of the internal features of eyes, nose, and mouth) are more difficult to detect than changes to isolated features (e.g. glasses or moustache) in inverted faces (Rhodes et al., 1993). Similarly, James Bartlett and Jean Searcy (Bartlett, 1994; Bartlett & Searcy, 1993; Searcy & Bartlett, in press) have shown that faces made to look grotesque by changing the spatial relations between parts no longer look grotesque when inverted, whereas faces whose grotesqueness depends on isolated feature cues (e.g. fangs added, eyes reddened) continue to look grotesque when inverted. These results support Diamond and Carey's claim that large inversion decrements are a hallmark of relational feature coding.

The most extreme form of relational feature coding is holistic coding, in which there is no explicit representation of parts at all. Perhaps faces are represented more holistically than other objects (Corballis, 1991; Farah, 1992; Farah, Tanaka, & Drain, 1995; Tanaka & Farah, 1993). If parts are not explicitly represented then they should be difficult to recognise in isolation. Therefore, the finding that parts are recognised better when presented in the whole object than in isolation, for faces but not for scrambled faces, inverted faces, or houses (Tanaka & Farah, 1993), suggests that upright faces are coded more holistically than these other classes of objects. Forcing people to code faces in terms of their parts, by presenting the head outline, eyes, nose, and mouth in separate frames, also eliminates the inversion decrement for faces (Farah et al., 1995). Farah and her colleagues therefore suggest that the disproportionate inversion decrement normally found for face recognition reflects holistic coding.

These results, however, are also consistent with the idea that relational features are crucial for face recognition. In the first case, the relationships between a target part and the rest of the face will be disrupted when that part is presented in isolation. In the second case, relational features will be difficult to code when the parts of a face are shown in separate frames. It should not be surprising if holistic and relational coding prove difficult to distinguish experimentally, because holistic coding is really an extreme form of relational coding.

Faces provide the most dramatic illustration of the homogeneity problem, but the ability to code variations in a shared configuration would be useful in many discriminations, ranging from biologically significant discriminations between different kinds of animals and plants, to more mundane discriminations between different cars or chairs. Therefore, relational coding could be part of a general solution to the homogeneity problem. Alternatively, it might be part of a special system dedicated to face recognition (for further discussion see Farah, 1992; Rhodes, 1994, 1996).

The idea that faces might be special has considerable appeal. There are neural areas dedicated to face recognition, damage to which results in prosopagnosia, a remarkably specific inability to recognise faces (for reviews see Damasio, Tranel & Damasio, 1990; de Renzi, 1986; Farah, 1990). The importance of faces may have generated considerable selection pressure for an efficient face recognition system, and evolution certainly seems to have equipped neonates with a built-in interest in faces (for a review see Johnson & Morton, 1991). Finally, the unusual homogeneity of faces may demand a special-purpose system for successful recognition.

Despite the plausibility of the idea, however, there is no evidence for a processing system that deals exclusively with faces (e.g. Diamond & Carey, 1986; Davidoff, 1986; Ellis & Young, 1989; Farah, 1992; Levine, 1989; Morton & Johnson, 1989; Rhodes, 1996). In particular, the coding of relational information that is so important for face recognition is not unique to faces. Diamond and Carey (1986) found an inversion decrement for recognising whole body profiles of dogs that was as large as the decrement for face recognition. The large inversion decrement for dog recognition was confined to dog experts, suggesting that expertise is needed to use relational features, presumably because subjects must learn which ones are relevant for the class. Moreover, the large inversion decrement for face recognition itself emerges gradually during childhood, as expertise with faces is acquired (for reviews see Carey, 1992; Carey & Diamond, 1994), and it is not found for faces from an unfamiliar racial group (Rhodes, Tan, Brake, & Taylor, 1989). In contrast, with sufficient expertise (e.g. after massive amounts of practice), even inverted faces can yield their relational features (Takane & Sergent, 1983). Therefore, faces may be special, but probably only because they are unusually homogeneous.

CARICATURES AND RECOGNITION

Diamond and Carey's analysis, and other similar proposals about how homogeneous objects are recognised (see Rhodes et al., 1993 for a review), emphasise the importance of spatial relations within the object. However, homogeneous classes offer another kind of spatial relationship that could be exploited to aid recognition. Because these objects share a configuration, they can be superimposed or averaged to produce a *norm* that captures the central tendency of the class, and each member of the class will differ from that norm in its own characteristic way. Whatever deviates from the norm becomes a critical feature for recognition. Now these norm-deviations are precisely what is exaggerated in a caricature, so the power of caricatures may well offer new clues about how the homogeneity problem is solved. In the following chapters I will attempt to uncover these clues.

ORGANISATION OF THE BOOK

I begin, in Chapter 2, with a close look at caricatures themselves—what they are, how they differ from cartoons, their potential to be superportraits, their relationship to norms and averages, and their invention and development by artists. In Chapter 3, I describe the recent development of computer programs that can be used to produce caricatures—programs that have become an essential tool for studying caricature recognition.

Although we associate caricatures primarily with artists, many animals also exploit the power of caricatures, using extreme traits or displays to influence their fellows. In Chapter 4, I examine the role of these supernormal stimuli in biological systems, asking why natural caricatures are so common and so effective. Part of the answer comes from studies of discrimination learning, reviewed in Chapter 5, which show that humans, other animals, and even computer recognition systems often respond strongly to stimuli that exaggerate the differences between the objects being distinguished. By focusing on the discrimination of simple stimuli that may differ on only a single dimension, such as wavelength or intensity, these "peak shift" studies have revealed important clues about how caricatures can be so powerful.

In Chapter 6, I feature the efforts of cognitive psychologists to assess the power of caricatures for more complex, spatially homogeneous stimuli like faces. Most of these studies use the computer caricature generators described in Chapter 3 to provide precise control over the level of exaggeration and the choice of norm(s). Their results corroborate the testimony of artists, animals, and the casual observer, that caricatures are highly recognisable, sometimes even more so than undistorted images.

In Chapter 7, I ask how such distorted images can be so effective. What mechanisms might account for the power of caricatures? I also examine whether or not caricatures exploit some special feature of the face recognition system and whether or not their effectiveness requires expertise. Finally, in Chapter 8, I offer some general conclusions about caricatures and recognition.

NOTES

1. Changes of illumination and changes within the object itself (bodies move, expressions change, etc.) can also alter the appearance of an object. However, I will limit this discussion to changes of viewpoint, because this is the problem that has received the most attention from researchers in visual cognition.
2. There are some dissenters (e.g. Cave & Kosslyn, 1993; Ullman, 1989).
3. Many similar distinctions have been made—isolated/configural, piecemeal/holistic, part-based/holistic, independent/interactive—all tapping the notion of a contrast between simple cues like parts and more complex spatial relations. See Rhodes, Brake, and Atkinson (1993) for a review.

CHAPTER TWO

The nature of caricature

Caricature is a graphical coding of facial features that seeks paradoxically to be more like a face than the face itself. It ... amplifies perceptually significant information while reducing less relevant details. The resulting distortion satisfies the beholder's mental model of what is unique about a particular face...

Brennan (1985) p.170

In this chapter I turn from broad theoretical questions about recognition and the challenge of caricatures, to consider caricatures themselves. What are their essential features? Can they reveal character as well as capturing a likeness? How do they differ from cartoons? I also examine the crucial role of norms in making caricatures. In the section on Caricatures in Art and Psychology I discuss how faces are a problem for artists, who want to capture a likeness, as well as for psychologists, who want to understand how we solve the homogeneity problem, and I suggest that the power of caricatures may illuminate both problems. Finally, I chart the progress of caricaturing from the Italian Renaissance to the computer age.

CHARACTERISING CARICATURES

Exaggeration and individuation

One of the earliest caricatures of a known individual is shown in Fig. 2.1 (Geipel, 1972). A pen and ink sketch by Gian Lorenzo Bernini (1598–1680), the baroque sculptor and architect, it depicts a decrepit figure propped up in bed, apparently wearing a large nightcap. In fact the nightcap is a mitre and the figure is Pope Innocent XI. The pope's most impressive feature is surely his nose, rendered in gargantuan proportions. Although Innocent XI does not seem to have inspired many portraits (only two are mentioned in Lane & Browne's *A.L.A. portrait index*, 1906), the one shown in Fig. 2.2 confirms that his nose was indeed distinctive! Setting aside the worry that the portrait might itself be a caricature, Bernini's drawing dramatically illustrates the essence of caricature, namely its *exaggeration of an individual's distinctive features*.

The term *caricature* comes from the Italian, *caricare*, meaning "to load", "surcharge", or "exaggerate". An early definition characterises caricatures as, "Those burlesque pictures, which the Italians call Caracatura's; where the Art consists in preserving, amidst distorted

FIG. 2.1. Caricature of Innocent XI by Gian Lorenzo Bernini. Reproduced with the permission of the Museum der Bildenden Künste. (Photograph: Museum der Bildenden Künste.)

FIG. 2.2. Medallion portrait of Innocent XI. Reproduced with the permission of the Vatican Library. (Photograph: Biblioteca Apostolica Vaticana, Medagliere.)

Proportions and aggravated Features, some distinguishing likeness of the Person" (Hughes, 1712, cited by OED). Current usage is similar. The *Oxford English Dictionary* defines caricature as the "grotesque or ludicrous representation of persons or things by exaggeration of their most characteristic and striking features", and the *Oxford Companion to Art* defines a caricature as "a 'charged' or 'loaded' portrait" (Osborne, 1970, p.203).

The term "caricature" is sometimes used more broadly to include the monstrous or absurd images known as grotesques (Fig. 2.3) and exaggerated types, such as the fool or the miser, that do not portray particular individuals (Chilvers, Osborne, & Farr, 1988). It has even been applied to the personification of nations, factions, or ideals (e.g. Wechsler, 1982), so that Uncle Sam, the Republican elephant and the Democratic donkey would count as caricatures. However, such a broad application is unusual and the term is usually restricted to "portrait-caricatures" that represent recognisable individuals (e.g. Gombrich & Kris, 1940; Osborne, 1970; Perkins, 1975).

The essential features of caricature therefore appear to be *exaggeration* and *individuation*: a caricature differs from a *realistic portrait* by its deliberate distortion, and from a *grotesque* by its representation of a known individual. Other features also commonly associated with the concept are a caricature's power to reveal true

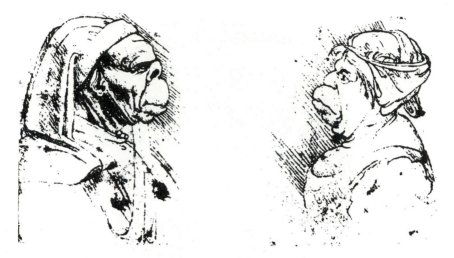

FIG. 2.3. Physiognomic sketches (detail) by Leonardo da Vinci. Reproduced with the permission of the Musée du Louvre. (Photograph: Agence photographique de la réunion des musées nationaux.)

character or personality, its focus on defects, its humour, and simplification. Let's consider each of these in turn.

Character revealed

A compelling aspect of caricature is its potential to highlight an individual's character or personality. For example, caricatures of Richard Nixon (Fig. 2.4) that exaggerate his ski-jump nose cleverly draw attention to an aspect of his character, at least to those familiar with the Pinocchio story![1] Annibale Carracci (1560–1609), who coined the term *caricature*, emphasised this power to reveal an individual's true *character*, which he contrasted with the classical portrait's power to capture true *form*. He asked rhetorically, "Is not the task of the Caricaturist exactly the same as that of the classical Artist? Both see the lasting truth behind the surface of mere outward appearance. Both try to help Nature accomplish its plan. The one may strive to visualize the perfect form and to realize it in his work, the other to grasp the perfect deformity, and thus reveal the very essence of a personality." (cited by Geipel, 1972, p.56).

Of course there is no guarantee that caricatures reveal *true* character, any more than faces themselves reflect a person's character. Many caricatures no doubt simply reinforce the erroneous or stereotyped attributions that we make on the basis of a person's appearance, and others may not offer any character analysis at all.

"THERE'S A HOLE IN THE BUCKET, DEAR HENRY, DEAR HENRY!"

FIG. 2.4. Caricature of Richard Nixon by Eric Heath. Reproduced with the artist's permission.

Exaggerating defects

A focus on defects was central to Carracci's notion of caricature and recurs in other early writings on the subject. For example, one writer suggested that portrait caricaturists "aim at the greatest resemblance of the whole of the person portrayed, while yet, for the purpose of fun, and sometimes of mockery, they disproportionately increase and emphasize the *defects* of the features they copy, so that the portrait as a whole appears to be the sitter himself while its component parts are changed" (my italics) (Baldinucci, 1681, cited by Gombrich & Kris, 1952, pp.189–190).

Today, we seem to adopt a more liberal criterion, considering the exaggeration of any distinctive features, defective or otherwise, as portrait caricature. However, the two views may not be so very different. Carracci and his seventeenth-century Italian contemporaries believed in Platonic ideals and the idea that individuals were mere imperfect copies of these underlying *true forms* or *ideals*. In this framework beauty depends on conformity to the ideal and *any* individuating feature is necessarily a defect, simply by virtue of its failure to conform to the ideal. Therefore, what would be distinctive features to us, would be defects to these neoclassicists. Moreover, a truly average face would be considered perfect and would be impossible to caricature.

Humour

A caricaturist's intent is often humorous and many caricatures are undoubtedly funny. It would be hard not to smile at Margaret Thatcher's image in Fig. 2.5. One source of the amusement is probably the paradoxical quality of caricatures, their accurate portrayal of a face's "trends" despite their obvious metric inaccuracy (Perkins, 1975). This juxtaposition and the surprise of recognising such a distorted image may trigger a smile. So, too, may witty visual allusions to non-visual characteristics—such as Thatcher's domineering style or Nixon's apparent penchant for lies. The contrast between a caricature's distortion and ideals of beauty and proportion may also provoke the laughter of embarrassment or fear (*Encyclopedia of world art*, 1960, p.763).

However, humour is not an inevitable feature of caricature. As the psychologist David Perkins (1975) pointed out, caricatures of Jews (really exaggerated types rather than portrait-caricatures) by Nazi propagandists were hardly amusing. Caricature and humour may be

FIG. 2.5. 3-D caricature of Margaret Thatcher by Peter Fluck and Roger Law. Reproduced with the permission of Spitting Image. (Photograph: Spitting Image.)

typically linked because exaggeration is a common humorous device, but exaggeration need not be humorous.

Simplification

Caricatures are usually drawings or engravings, which are *simpler* than other forms of portraiture. In a literal sense, these graphic forms are impoverished. By relying on line, they lack information about colour and shading contained in a painting or photograph. However, simplification can be a powerful tool for conveying visual information. Gombrich (1960) cites the success of portraits by Rembrandt where the eyes are in shadow and gold braid is rendered in a single brush-stroke, to show that the most successful representations may be simplified or ambiguous. Indeed, Gombrich conjectured that too much detail in portraits may be responsible for the frozen, expressionless look so often found in realistic paintings and photographs.

Simplification works, according to Gombrich, because it facilitates the viewer's contribution, the "beholder's share". As the artist Sir Joshua Reynolds (1723–1792) observed, "From a slight under-determined drawing, where the ideas of the composition and characters are ... only touched upon, the imagination supplies more than the painter himself could possibly produce; and we accordingly often find that the finished work disappoints the expectation that was raised from the sketch" (cited by Lucie-Smith, 1981, p.59). Of course considerable skill is needed to know what to retain, and there must be no blatant contradiction that prevents the illusion from taking shape (Gombrich, 1960). The disruptive effects of such contradictions have been confirmed in a study of caricatures of Richard Nixon (Perkins, 1975). Even the simplest caricatures were effective so long as no key feature (elongated nose, box chin, jowls, and hairline with bays) was wrongly represented or "contra-indicated". Omitting a feature completely was much less disruptive than getting it wrong.

Clearly then, simplification can be more effective than a deliberate attempt to include all the details of a visual scene. Indeed, part of the power of caricatures may lie in their selectivity about what is represented. However, unlike exaggeration, simplification is not essential to caricature, because caricatures can be very detailed, as illustrated in Fig. 2.5.[2]

Caricatures and cartoons

No discussion of the nature of caricatures would be complete without some mention of how they differ from cartoons. Originally, cartoons were drawings used to transfer an artist's design to a painting, tapestry, or stained glass panel. However, these are not the cartoons with which caricatures are often confused. Rather, the confusion is with the kind of humorous or satirical drawings popularised by Punch magazine in the nineteenth century. Their first cartoon, published in 1843[3], was a send-up of an exhibition of fresco-cartoons entered in a competition to decorate the Houses of Parliament (Horn, 1980; Osborne, 1970). It appeared under the heading "Cartoon" and the label stuck.

Cartoons and caricatures often look alike, both typically being graphic forms that rely primarily on line to depict figures or objects. Moreover, caricatures often feature in cartoons. However, despite their superficial similarity and the fact that the terms are sometimes used interchangeably, caricatures and cartoons are different. They differ in both their aims and their devices. The point of a cartoon is to express an *idea*, preferably in as witty and memorable a manner as possible (McCutcheon, 1950, cited by Horn, 1980; Westwood, 1932). For example, Eric Heath's cartoon in Fig. 2.4 suggests that Nixon and Kissinger are not happy with the impact of Australian and New Zealand Labour governments on US foreign policy in the South Pacific. The use of caricatures of Nixon and Kissinger no doubt contributes to its impact, but the caricatures themselves have the more limited goal of depicting (and perhaps commenting on) *individuals*. Caricatures are simply one of many devices used by the cartoonist (e.g. symbols, verbal labels, etc. See Gombrich, 1963 for an analysis of the "cartoonist's armory").

Caricatures as superportraits

Annibale Carracci believed that, "A good caricature, like every work of art, is more true to life than reality itself" (cited by Geipel, 1972, p.56), because of its power to reveal a person's true character. However, an even more intriguing possibility is that a caricature could capture a person's true *appearance*. Perhaps lengthening Nixon's already long nose would result in a *superportrait* that was more like Nixon than Nixon himself (Fig. 2.4). Several psychologists have suggested that this may be possible—that exaggeration might, "heighten(s) the real and significant appearance of an individual" (Gordon, 1989, p.166), and that, despite its distortion, a caricature, "may be faithful to those features of the man that distinguish him from all other men and thus may truly represent him in a higher sense of the term. It may correspond to him in the sense of being uniquely specific to him—more so than a projective drawing or photographic portrait would be" (J.J. Gibson, 1971, p.29). This question of whether caricatures can be superportraits and, if so, what this would tell us about recognition, is a major focus of this book.

CARICATURES AS DEVIATIONS FROM A NORM

Implicit in the notion of caricature as the exaggeration of distinctive information is the concept of a norm or reference point against which the exaggeration occurs. Perkins (1975, p.7) makes this explicit when he defines a caricature as, "a symbol that exaggerates measurements relative to individuating norms". Thus the "exaggeration" of a caricature amplifies whatever it is about the face that differs from the norm. An unusually large nose will grow, but unusually small eyes will shrink. Therefore, although metrically inaccurate, a caricature may accurately describe a face's "trends".

Many different kinds of norm can be used to generate caricatures. The earliest caricatures were exaggerations relative to an ideal, from which any deviation was seen as a defect (see Perkins, 1975). They were attempts to capture *la perfetta deformità*, the perfect deformity, and caricaturists were fascinated with the notion of "ideal ugliness" in contrast to the focus of serious Renaissance art on "ideal beauty". An early "how-to" book, *Rules for drawing caricaturas*, published in 1788, describes this kind of caricature, "The sculptors of Ancient Greece seem to have diligently observed the forms and proportions constituting the European idea of beauty ... These measures are to be met with in many drawing books; a slight deviation from them, by the predominancy of any feature, constitutes what is called *character* ... this deviation or peculiarity, aggravated, forms *caricatura*" (Grose, cited in Horn, 1980, p.15). To create such a caricature, the caricaturist would choose some ideal of beauty as the norm.

The best kind of norm for creating a recognisable portrait caricature is probably an average face that captures the central tendency of the population (or some relevant subset, such as young, female faces). Each face has its own peculiar set of deviations from such an average and by exaggerating these deviations, the caricaturist can highlight what makes that face unique.

The caricaturist's average face exists in the mind's eye, if it exists at all in any explicit form. However, real images of average faces can also be created. Charles Darwin's cousin Francis Galton was the first to make composite or average faces. In 1878 he invented a multiple-exposure photography technique, which he used to average the faces of various groups: family members, criminals, consumptives, and even vegetarians (see Fig. 2.6)! Galton was caught up in the Victorian enthusiasm for physiognomy and his goal was to capture facial types, such as the criminal type. Unfortunately, he failed to find the criminal type by averaging criminals' faces, a procedure that generated a surprisingly benign face. Instead he discovered that averages were attractive. This

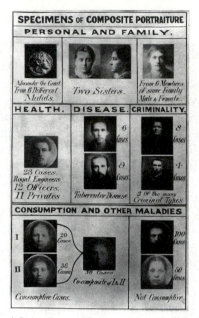

FIG. 2.6. Examples of Galton's portrait composites (Galton, 1883).

discovery confirmed an earlier observation about the effect of blending faces in a stereoscope, described in a letter to Galton from A.L. Austin of Invercargill, New Zealand. Austin wrote that, "the faces blend into one in a most remarkable manner, producing in the case of some ladies' portraits, in every instance, a *decided improvement* in beauty" (Galton, 1878, p.137).

Averageness and attractiveness

The attractiveness of average faces has been confirmed recently using a computerised version of Galton's photographic averaging technique (Fig. 2.7). Judith Langlois and her colleagues (Langlois & Roggman, 1990; Langlois, Roggman, & Musselman, 1994) demonstrated that computer-averaged composites were more attractive than the component faces. In fact the more faces that went into the composites, the more attractive they became. Some commentators have worried that the attractiveness of these averages may simply be an artifact of their soft-focus look and smooth skin texture (Benson & Perrett, 1992; Pittenger, 1991). However, line-drawing averages, which avoid these problems, are also considered more attractive than the component faces, and the attractiveness of individual line-drawn faces is strongly related

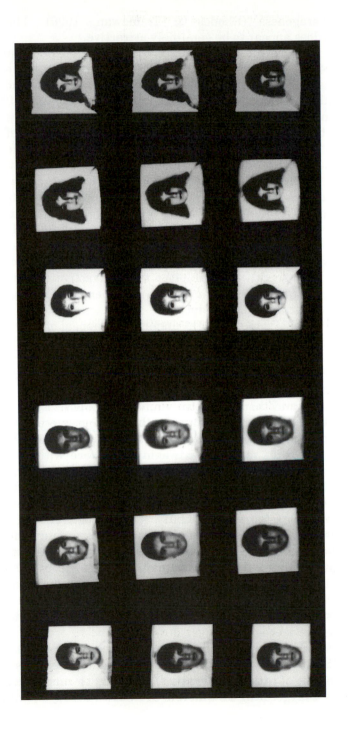

FIG. 2.7. Langlois and Roggman's computer-generated composite faces. From top to bottom in each column are composites of four, eight, sixteen, and thirty-two faces. Reprinted from *Psychological Science*, 1990, *1*, p.117 with permission. (Photograph: Judith Langlois.)

to their averageness (Rhodes & Tremewan, 1996). Therefore, averageness does appear to be genuinely attractive.

Just why average faces are attractive remains an open question (Etcoff, 1994). Our notions of beauty almost certainly have some biological basis, with adults in different cultures showing considerable agreement about what is attractive (see Langlois & Roggman, 1990 for a review) and infants as young as 2 months of age showing similar preferences to adults (Langlois et al., 1987). Therefore, our preference for averages may not simply be a product of cultural dictates. However, the exact biological mechanisms that make average faces attractive remain the subject of debate. One possibility is that evolutionary pressures have operated against facial extremes, making it adaptive to prefer averages. This kind of *stabilising selection* generally occurs when a trait has reached a stable, optimal value in a population. However, there is no independent evidence that this is true of the human facial configuration (Barash, 1982; Dobzhansky, 1970). Furthermore, extreme traits, like the peacock's tail, are often very attractive and, in these cases, selection pressures favour extremes rather than averages (for more detailed discussion see Chapter 4).

A preference for symmetry might underlie the appeal of averageness (Alley & Cunningham, 1991; Ridley, 1992), because composite faces are more symmetric than their component faces (Grammer & Thornhill, 1994). Langlois and her colleagues argue against this view, on the grounds that symmetry and attractiveness were uncorrelated in their sample of faces, and that perfectly symmetric composites, created by reflecting each half of the face across the midline, were much less attractive than the original faces (Langlois, et al., 1994). Perfectly symmetric composites made by averaging each face with its mirror image may also be less attractive than the original faces (Swaddle & Cuthill, 1995). In my lab, however, we have found that these perfectly symmetric composites are more attractive than the original faces, and that symmetry correlates significantly with attractiveness (Rhodes, Proffitt, Grady, & Sumich, in prep.). Moreover, we could reduce the attractiveness of faces by reducing their symmetry (i.e. exaggerating how each face differed from the symmetric composite by 50%), and increase attractiveness by increasing symmetry (i.e. reducing differences from the symmetric composite by 50%). These results suggest that a preference for symmetry could indeed contribute to the attractiveness of averageness.

Average faces are attractive, but they may not be the most attractive faces. In a recent *Nature* paper, David Perrett and his colleagues showed that a composite of attractive female faces could be made even more attractive by exaggerating its differences from an average female face

(Perrett, May, & Yoshikawa, 1994). Therefore, extreme versions of traits that are attractive in female faces may be more attractive than the original traits. The attractive composite had larger eyes, higher cheekbones, a smaller jaw, and shorter distances between the mouth and chin and between the nose and mouth, than the average female face. Other studies have found that large eyes, full lips, small noses, and small chins are attractive in female faces (Berry & Zebrowitz-McArthur, 1988; Cunningham, 1986), and that big eyes and chins are attractive in male faces (Cunningham, Barbee, & Pike, 1990). In general, however, exaggeration is not attractive in faces. Caricaturing a face almost always reduces its attractiveness, whereas making a face more average, by anticaricaturing it, almost invariably increases its attractiveness (Rhodes & Tremewan, 1996).

Caricatures were originally seen as deviations from an ideal, and hence as images that exaggerated a person's defects. Galton's discovery that average faces are attractive raises the intriguing possibility that caricatures can capture an individual's "perfect deformity" and their unique appearance *at the same time*. If averages are indeed attractive, then using an average as the norm may amount to the same thing as using an ideal of beauty as the norm, and the resulting caricatures will exaggerate both the individuality and ugliness of each face!

CARICATURES IN ART AND PSYCHOLOGY

In Chapter 1 I argued that the similarity of faces presents a problem for the visual system and for psychologists trying to understand how recognition works. It also creates a problem for artists trying to capture a facial likeness. Conventional portrait painters are all too familiar with complaints that they haven't got it quite right, and few have the confidence to respond as one painter did; "this painting, my dear Sir, resembles you more than you do yourself" (Gombrich, 1972, p.46).

One problem is the face's mobility (Gombrich 1960, 1972). Faces move about, so that we see them from a variety of perspectives, and expressions deform the surface. Yet the artist must capture a likeness in a static image. Even photographs may seem, "odd, uncharacteristic, strange, not because the camera distorts, but because [they catch] a constellation of features from the melody of expression which, when arrested and frozen, fails to strike us in the same way the sitter does. For expression in life and physiognomic impression rest on movement no less than on static symptoms, and art has to compensate for the loss of the time dimension by concentrating all required information into one arrested image" (Gombrich, 1960, p.292). If we are not aware of a face's instantaneous appearance in normal perception, then the frozen image of the artist or the camera may not satisfy us. Just as the correct disposition of the legs of a galloping horse, revealed by photography, had escaped observation, so too may the instantaneous appearances of a face.

Mobility, however, is not the only source of difficulty. Even static images of faces are difficult to reproduce. The portraits of queens and presidents on coins and bank notes are there as much to frustrate forgers as to satisfy patriotic instincts. Part of the problem lies in our exquisite sensitivity to variations in the basic facial configuration. This sensitivity allows us to recognise thousands of different faces, but it is not matched by an insight into the cues that support these discriminations. The configural cues that mediate successful recognition (Bartlett & Searcy, 1993; Diamond & Carey, 1986; Rhodes, 1988; Rhodes et al., 1993; Young, Hellawell, & Hay, 1987) and successful portraits (Gombrich, 1960) are not easily discovered by observation. Close scrutiny of faces does not reveal the requirements for a successful portrait, any more than it discloses how we solve the homogeneity problem. Therefore, artists had to *discover* how to make a convincing facial likeness, not by studying faces but by experimenting with pictorial effects. They had to examine the effect of variations in images on observers, much as psychologists do when studying object and face recognition. Töpffer's explorations on the facial expressions of doodles (Fig. 2.8) exemplify this empirical

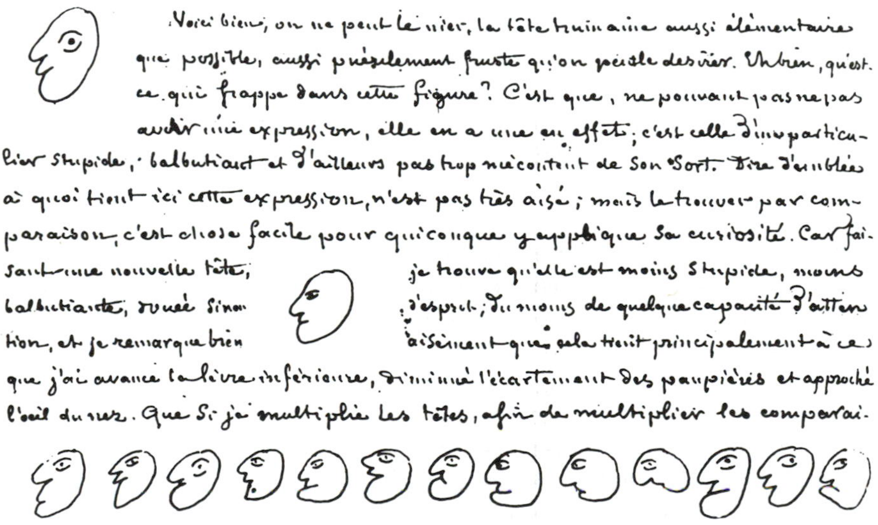

FIG. 2.8. Töpffer's face doodles. Reproduced with permission of Phaidon Press Ltd.

approach. Just as artists had to discover effects that would create an illusion of depth in pictures, so they also had to discover effects that would create an illusion of physiognomic likeness.

A more fundamental question is what constitutes a successful illusion of likeness. Gombrich has an appealing answer to this question. He conjectures that mimesis (mimicry) in art depends not on *resemblance*, but on the *generation of equivalent responses*.[4] A successful portrait "is not necessarily a replica of anything seen" (Gombrich, 1960, p.292). It need not resemble the original at all. But what it must do is evoke a response that is similar to the one evoked by what it represents. The success of caricatures provides dramatic evidence for this view. The inventors of portrait caricature discovered that these distorted images could evoke "equivalent" or even heightened responses without resembling the original in any straightforward way. This discovery and the subsequent artistic development of caricatures are the focus of the next section.

A BRIEF HISTORY OF CARICATURE[5]

Distortions of physical characteristics and expressions appear to be as old as art itself. Examples occur in prehistoric times and in the art of early Egyptian and Mesopotamian civilisations (*Encyclopedia of world art*, 1960). The tragic and comic masks worn in Greek theatre were grossly exaggerated, and medieval cathedrals housed almost as many grotesques and gargoyles as they did biblical figures. However, genuine caricatures, deliberate distortions of known individuals, are not found until much later. One of the earliest is a thirteenth-century ink drawing of Isaac of Norwich and two other wealthy Jews, shown in the company of devils (Fig. 2.9). Apparently, the use of caricatures as propaganda goes back a long way.

Funny faces in the Italian Renaissance
Despite such occasional earlier examples, it was not until the end of the sixteenth century that the notion of portrait-caricature was articulated and clear examples are found. Annibale Carracci, an Italian painter in the "grand manner", is recognised as the first genuine caricaturist (Fig. 2.10). As already noted, he coined the term *caricatura* and defended the artistic integrity of the enterprise. The technique caught on and many other respected Italian artists experimented with caricaturing. A beautifully economical example is Bernini's caricature of Cardinal Scipio Borghese (Fig. 2.11), the success of which can be judged by comparison with his sculpture of the cardinal (Fig. 2.12). By the

FIG. 2.9. An early caricature appearing in a *Rotulus Judeorum* in 1233. Reproduced with the permission of the Public Record Office.

eighteenth century, the Italian artist Pier Leone Ghezzi (1674–1755) was even able to make a living as a caricaturist, with witty but sympathetic caricatures (Gombrich & Kris, 1940).

Given that distortion featured in art from the earliest times, why should caricature have made such a late entrance on the artistic scene? The art historians Sir Ernst Gombrich and Ernst Kris (1940) speculate that there was a taboo against distorting the image of an individual during the Classical period. They note that, "Classical art has preserved innumerable comic types of old slaves and amusing parasites, but not a single caricature of an individual. To distort the image of an individual was, as it were, taboo; the comic might not intrude on civic dignity" (op.cit., p.6). Later, they suggest that the hegemony of the early Christian church over art ensured that caricature did not emerge in the Middle Ages either. Art became a didactic tool for the church, and distortion was used to highlight the plight of "generic" sinners. Political propagandists used cruder means than portrait-caricature to make their point. Typically the enemy was simply hung in effigy and these defamatory images could be offered as security for loans, to be displayed

FIG. 2.10. Annibale Carracci's caricature of a singer and his wife. Reproduced with the permission of the Statens Konstmuseer. (Photograph: Statens Konstmuseer.)

if the debtor defaulted (Gombrich, 1963). This practice exploited a widespread belief in the power of images. Gombrich and Kris (1940, p.15) speculate, "Before caricature as an art could be born, mankind had to become mentally free enough to accept this distortion of an image as an artistic achievement and not as a dangerous practice". Perhaps by the end of the Renaissance, people were liberated enough from such superstitions for caricatures to have popular appeal. Vestiges of these old beliefs in the power of images may, however, still be with us. For example, Salman Rushdie's *Satanic verses* provoked not only a death sentence, but also a call for a caricature competition, from his enemies. Apparently they sought to mutilate his image as well as his person.

It was only at the end of the Italian Renaissance that artists began to reject realist constraints. Gombrich and Kris (1940, p.15) propose that, "the artist had to learn ... that in painting an individual he was under no necessity to produce an exact likeness, but was free to express

FIG. 2.11. Gian Lorenzo Bernini's caricature of Cardinal Scipio Borghese. Reproduced with the permission of the Vatican Library. (Photograph: Vatican Library.)

his personal vision of the sitter's essential characteristics". These artists were certainly not as liberated as Salvador Dali (1904–1989), who claimed that he didn't paint portraits to look like his subjects but that his subjects grew to look like his portraits. Their experiments with caricature may, however, have helped make such a view possible.

Carracci's own views on portrait caricature offer another clue as to why the enterprise emerged when it did. He and other early caricaturists believed that by exaggerating a person's distinctive features, they could capture that person's true character. This view fits well with the physiognomic thesis, popular at the time, that outward appearance reflects inner character. Animal analogies were a popular source of these character attributions, with the (supposed) characteristics of particular animals attributed to people resembling that animal. These ideas persist in contemporary descriptions of people as "mousy", "catty", "a cold fish", "looking sheepish", as being "a cunning

FIG. 2.12. Gian Lorenzo Bernini's bust of Cardinal Scipio Borghese. Reproduced with the permission of the Galleria Borghese.

little monkey", or a "sly fox", and animal analogies continue to amuse us (Fig. 2.13).

Physiognomy, the view that character is displayed in appearance, goes back to antiquity, influencing Islamic as well as Western thought (Baltrusaitis, 1989). However, it received a major boost at the end of the sixteenth century, with a small explosion of books on the "science" of physiognomy. The best known of these was *De Humana Physiognomia*, by Carracci's contemporary, Giambattista della Porta (1541–1615). It contained numerous woodcuts of face–animal analogies, highlighting resemblances between human and animal faces (Fig. 2.14). As it was published in Naples in 1586, Carracci would almost certainly have seen it. Gombrich (1963, p.205) suggests that these "visual equations" would have "demonstrated to the discerning artist how little the impression of likeness depended on an accurate mapping of the sitter's features. A few strokes might suffice to catch a characteristic expression and yet transform the man into an animal". Thus, the popularity of physiognomy may have given portrait caricature a boost, by showing that a likeness can be preserved in the context of exaggeration, and by

FIG. 2.13. Human–animal analogies. Copyright *France-Dimanche*, April 9, 1950. Reproduced with permission.

FIG. 2.14. Human–animal analogies by Giambattista della Porta.

its intriguing implication that such exaggeration could also reveal a person's true character.

Send-ups: Caricature and satire in eighteenth-century England

By the eighteenth century, the action had shifted from Italy to England, where William Hogarth (1697–1764) combined Italian portrait-caricature with Dutch genre painting to produce lively social commentaries (Lucie-Smith, 1981). Despite producing many caricatures, however, Hogarth was a reluctant caricaturist, dismissing the art as, "a species of lines that are produced rather by the hand of chance than of skill" (cited by Antal, 1962, p.135). According to the art historian Antal, Hogarth saw himself as "a painter of characters, a psychological painter, a 'comic history painter', and not as a mere caricaturist" (p.133). In fact Hogarth's famous "Characters and Caricaturas" (Fig. 2.15) was designed precisely to distinguish his "character" painting from caricature. At the bottom of the main picture of over 100 heads, Hogarth added caricatures by Leonardo da Vinci (actually a grotesque; bottom right), Annibale Carracci (second from right), and Pier Leone Ghezzi (fourth from left). He also included several more realistic images by Raphael, to show that his own heads, displayed in the main body of the picture, resembled these much more than they resembled the caricatures.

Hogarth was fascinated by physiognomy and facial expression. Like Carracci, he almost certainly knew della Porta's work (Antal, 1962). In his youth he sketched prominent facial features (possibly caricatured!) on his fingernails (Antal, 1962) and in his later years he wrote extensively about facial expressions (both their muscular basis and their implications for character) in *The analysis of beauty* (1753). However, Hogarth was no knee-jerk physiognomist and he warned against hasty judgments of character based merely on expression, because the same "aspect" could have different causes (Antal, 1962).

Other eighteenth-century English caricaturists included George, Marquess of Townshend (1724–1807), who circulated caricatures of his political colleagues and rivals (Gombrich, 1963), Thomas Rowlandson (1756–1827), who earned enough from caricaturing to support a notorious gambling habit (Chilvers et al., 1988), and James Gillray (1757–1815), who turned portrait-caricature into a political weapon (Lucie-Smith, 1981). Gillray's powerful images (e.g. Fig. 2.16) attracted crowds to the London print shop where they were displayed. One witness commented, "the enthusiasm is indescribable when the next drawing appears; it is a veritable madness. You have to make your way in through the crowd with your fists" (cited by Hillier, 1970, p.47).

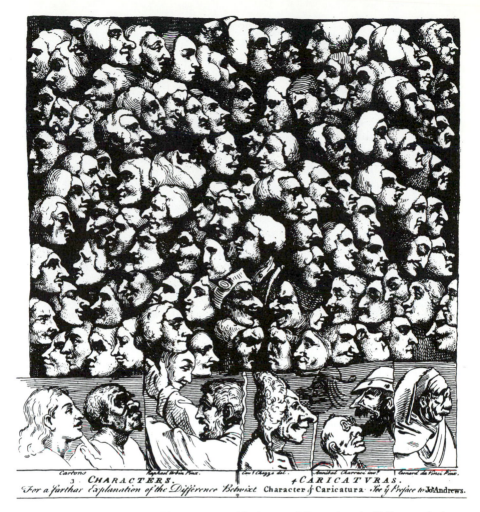

FIG. 2.15. William Hogarth's "Characters and Caricaturas". Reproduced with the permission of the Whitworth Art Gallery, University of Manchester. (Photograph: The Whitworth Art Gallery.)

Put-downs: Caricature and political struggle in nineteenth-century France

One of the most intense political campaigns featuring caricatures was waged in the Parisian mass media[6] in the 1830s, when Charles Philipon's (1800–1862) *La Caricature* (1830–1835) and *Le Charivari*[7] (1832–1842) campaigned against the new King Louis-Philippe (a detailed account is provided by Wechsler, 1982). Louis-Philippe was installed as a constitutional monarch when Charles X was overthrown

FIG. 2.16. James Gillray's "The Plum Pudding is in Danger".

during the July revolution of 1830, France's second revolution in just over 40 years. However, his popularity was short-lived, as shown by Honoré-Victorin Daumier's (1808–1879) scatological *La Gargantua* (Fig. 2.17), published by Philipon in 1831. Louis-Philippe was not amused and Daumier spent six months in prison.

However, the press was not deterred, and resorted to subtler means when the censorship laws, ironically abolished after the 1830 revolution, became more repressive. Under pressure from the censors, Philipon invented *"la poire"* (the pear) as an emblem for Louis-Philippe. Subtle enough to escape suppression initially, the pear was a clever device, referring not only to Louis-Philippe's pear-like appearance, but also mocking him, *"la poire"* being slang for "fathead". On 14 November 1831, however, Philipon was prosecuted (as on many other occasions, Ramus, 1978). In his defence he produced the now-famous pear series (Fig. 2.18), in which he gradually transformed Louis-Philippe into a pear, and argued that, to be consistent, all pear-like images would have to be banned. The censors agreed and pears were banned! Still defiant, Philipon printed the censors' ruling against him on the front page of *La Caricature* in the shape of a pear. Then, in 1835, the government banned the expression of ideas in drawings, while upholding the right to publish

FIG. 2.17. Henri Daumier's "Gargantua".

the opinions themselves, and *La Caricature* was finished. The authorities realised that caricatures were more powerful than words in a city where half the population was illiterate (Wechsler, 1982). All direct references to individuals and institutions were outlawed, and artists like Daumier were forced away from portrait caricature, back to social satire populated with generic types and invented characters like Robert Macaire, the arch swindler and con-man who personified Louis-Philippe's exploitative regime.

By this time, physiognomy had been further systematised and popularised by Charles Le Brun (1702). Johann Caspar Lavater (1789) had invented the transformation technique used so effectively in *Les Poires*, although he preferred to transform humans into animals. The result was a widespread craze for physiognomy and facial types (Cowling, 1989; Wechsler, 1982). Sir Francis Galton's experiments with composite portraits, described earlier, were an attempt to capture the "criminal", the "officer", and other facial types. Even Charles Dickens was swept along on this physiognomic tide, asserting that the facial features of one convicted murderer "might have afforded sufficient grounds for his instant execution at any time, even had there been no other evidence against him" (cited by Cowling, 1989, p.309)! How such an audience must have relished the efforts of caricaturists who exploited this physiognomic philosophy.

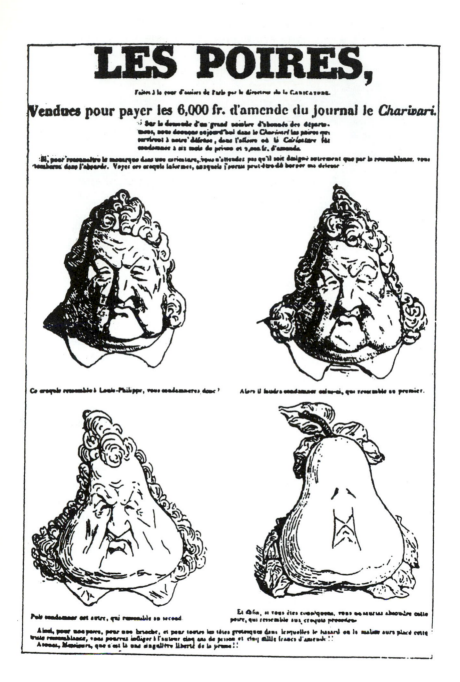

FIG. 2.18. Charles Philipon's "*Les Poires*".

The demise of physiognomy: Twentieth-century caricatures

Contemporary caricatures operate largely outside the framework of physiognomy, animal analogies, and facial types that dominated nineteenth-century caricaturing. Physiognomy is no longer popular or scientifically respectable. "Character" undoubtedly has some impact on facial appearance (e.g. characteristic facial expressions can leave permanent traces, such as frown lines and smile lines, that provide some cues to a person's disposition), but we recognise that facial traits have multiple causes so that the face is not a very reliable guide to character (see Zebrowitz, 1996, for further discussion). The appeal of today's caricatures must rely more on the clever rendering of likeness out of unlikeness and less on the idea that they reveal a person's true character.

Daily newspapers have replaced the satirical magazines of the nineteenth century (e.g. *Harper's Weekly* in the US; *La Caricature* and *Le Charivari* in France; *Punch* in England; *Simplicissimus* and *Kladderadatsch* in Germany) as the main outlet for caricaturists and cartoonists. Despite the pressures to uniformity inherent in mass media, a tremendous diversity of styles remains, from the carefully designed and cross-hatched drawings of David Levine to the raw power of Fluck and Law's 3-D models (Fig. 2.5).

Caricatures in the computer age: Approaching the twenty-first century

The most radical and exciting development in recent times is the use of computers to generate caricatures. Now even the least skilled among us can create convincing caricatures. More importantly, by allowing precise control over the degree of distortion and the choice of norm, these computer caricaturists provide a vital tool for researchers attempting to understand the power of caricatures. In the next chapter I will lay some groundwork for the discussion of that work in Chapters 6 and 7, by describing how computers create caricatures.

NOTES

1. Pinocchio was a wooden puppet with a long nose, which grew even longer when he told a lie. Nixon has also been likened to Pinocchio in a comic monologue by David Frye, "Richard Nixon Superstar" (discussed by Grofman, 1989).
2. Actually some degree of simplification may be inevitable in any kind of portrait, caricatured or otherwise. One commentator notes that, "In portraiture, whether painting or drawing, the artist has to decide what is essential, and to leave out what is unessential. He *cannot* put down all

he sees ... every artist and every portrait painter must select, and must reject what is not characteristic" (Kapp, cited by Westwood, 1932, p. 130).

3.   Earlier satirical drawings had appeared since 1841, but under the rather uninspired heading, "Punch's pencilling".

4.   This view has the advantage of avoiding notorious philosophical problems with the notion of resemblance as an explanation of representation (for a more detailed discussion of the problem of representation see Cummins, 1989).

5.   This brief survey focuses on the development of portrait-caricature in European art. However, caricature is certainly not limited to Western art (see e.g. *Encyclopedia of world art*).

6.   The invention of lithography in 1798 allowed drawings to be easily mass produced. This technique of drawing on a limestone slab with a grease crayon also allowed a greater tonal range (from silvery greys to dark blacks) than other print media (Ramus, 1978). Colour lithography was developed in the 1870s.

7.   The term signifies a "noisy, jangling, mock serenade intended to harass an unliked party" (Ramus, 1978, p.xiii).

CHAPTER THREE

Caricatures by computer

*... what I really wanted was an algorithm that would enable
me to exaggerate a whole face dynamically and in parallel,
as I do in my imagination. This fantasy led me to write the
Caricature Generator software...*

Brennan (1985) p.172

THE CARICATURE GENERATOR

In 1982 Susan Brennan submitted a thesis for the Master of Science in
Visual Studies at MIT, in which she described *Caricature Generator*, a
computer program that creates caricatures (Brennan, 1982). An amateur
caricaturist herself (e.g. Fig. 3.1), she decided to automate the process
she used to create a caricature, which was to picture the whole face all
at once without analysing any one part of it and then watch it amplify
itself. Unfortunately, such a holistic, parallel exaggeration of the entire
face is disrupted by the serial process of drawing, which distracts the
artist from the whole. The goal of the Caricature Generator was to free
caricaturing from this seriality constraint and the motor skills required.

The Caricature Generator has been described in detail in *Leonardo*
(Brennan, 1985) and in *Scientific American* (Dewdney, 1986). Briefly, it
exaggerates distinctive aspects of a face relative to a norm, in three
steps. First, a photograph of a face is digitised, and a fixed set of 169

FIG. 3.1. Caricature of Gerald Ford by Susan Brennan.

landmark points are found by eye and marked using the mouse. This step could be automated, but point-finding on faces is a difficult computational problem in itself and has yet to be solved. The points were chosen to provide a recognisable image of a face using as few lines as possible, but including those lines typically drawn by caricaturists. They represent important spatial properties of a face such as its outline, the location and shape of internal features (eyes, nose, mouth), material changes (from hair to skin), and light/dark transitions produced by shadows on a 3-D face. The points are joined automatically by 37 spline (smooth) curves to produce a line drawing that is essentially a tracing of the photograph (Fig. 3.2). If a particular line segment is occluded (e.g. an ear) or absent from a face (e.g. the cheek lines in Fig. 3.2), it need not be displayed.

Having created a line drawing with human assistance, the program then takes control of the caricaturing process. In the second step, it compares the line drawing with that of a norm or average face, in order to determine what is distinctive about the face. The question of what norm to use is of both psychological and artistic significance. An artist

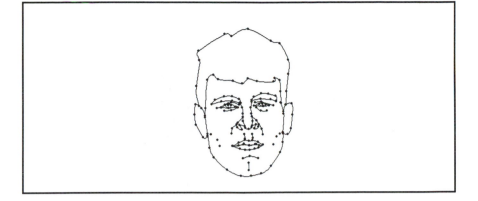

FIG. 3.2. A line drawing produced by the Caricature Generator. The 169 points used to describe the face are also displayed.

might be interested in deviations from a typical face, from a beautiful face, or from their own face (if the stories of artists' egos are to be believed). A psychologist might choose a norm that gives perceptually relevant distortions, such as an average of a set of faces of the same sex and race as the target. Caricaturing Caucasian faces against a Chinese norm, for example, would be unlikely to produce recognisable caricatures, because it would emphasise how Chinese faces differ from Caucasian faces rather than how they differ from each other. The Caricature Generator will use any norm specified by the user, provided it has the same number of points and the same line segment structure as the image to be caricatured, and so can be used to explore the effectiveness of different norms.

In the third and final step, all the metric differences between the face and the norm are exaggerated (the face and the norm are first scaled and translated so that their pupils are aligned). The program finds corresponding points on the face and the norm, represents the difference between these pairs of points as a vector, and increases the length of the vector by a specified constant proportion, thereby shifting the face-point further from its corresponding norm-point. For example, a 50% caricature is created by increasing the length of all vectors by 50%. This procedure has the effect of selectively exaggerating distinctive aspects of the face: 50% of a big difference will shift a point much further from the norm than will the same factor applied to a small difference. Anticaricatures can also be created by reducing the differences between the face-points and their corresponding norm-points. Using this software, one can produce a range of images for a face, as shown in Fig. 3.3. If desired, these plain drawings can then be enhanced using a

Undistorted Drawing

0%

Anti-caricatures

Caricatures

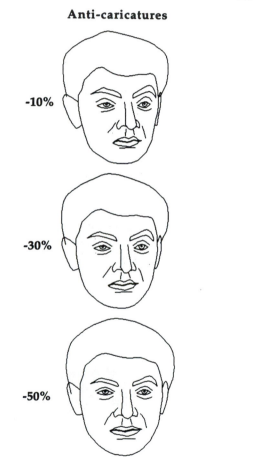

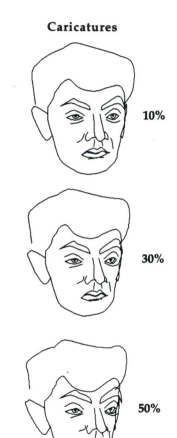

-10%

10%

-30%

30%

-50%

50%

FIG. 3.3. A set of caricatures and anticaricatures of Rowan Atkinson produced using the Caricature Generator.

Undistorted Drawing

0%

Anti-caricatures	Caricatures

-10% 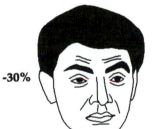 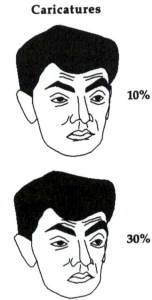 10%

-30% 30%

-50% 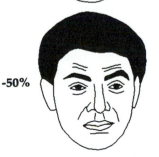 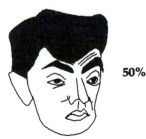 50%

FIG. 3.4. Enhanced drawings of Rowan Atkinson.

package like Superpaint to fill in the hair, eyebrows, and irises, as shown in Fig. 3.4.

Figure 3.5 shows some caricatures of famous faces produced in our laboratory using the Caricature Generator. There are certainly differences between these caricatures and those produced by human artists. Whereas artists may omit non-distinctive elements entirely, the Caricature Generator simply exaggerates less where the differences between the face and the norm are less. Also, the lines on these drawings can move into impossible configurations (e.g. an eyebrow can move down to cross an eye). Nevertheless, they have a vitality comparable to that of "real" caricatures and seem recognisable enough to warrant closer study (see Chapter 6).

BRENNAN'S COMPUTATIONAL THEORY OF CARICATURE

Brennan notes that it is extremely difficult to determine the key features for caricaturing or recognising a face, because they may vary from context to context, viewer to viewer, and, most importantly, from face to face. Therefore, she based the Caricature Generator on the idea that a caricaturist uses whatever is unique about a face. Assumptions about the generally important aspects of faces are implicit in the choice of points and lines used to represent a face, but beyond this there is no assumption that certain features are more important than any others and the idea (Brennan, 1985, p.173) is simply:

> to exaggerate the metric differences between a graphic representation of a subject face and some other similarly structured face, ideal or norm ... The critical process of selecting what to include and what to leave out (which comes so naturally to the human caricaturist) is finessed by having the computer exaggerate all spatial relationships and by delegating responsibility for choosing the basis for comparison to the human user of the system. Thus the system makes no qualitative decisions about individual distinctive features ... Implicit in the theory behind the Caricature Generator, then, is the convenient notion that a relationship between lines on the subject face becomes a 'feature' only when it differs significantly from the corresponding relationship on a comparison face—in other words, when it becomes useful in distinguishing one face from another.

PRINCE CHARLES

CARY GRANT

MARLON BRANDO

LEONARD BREZHNEV

CLINT EASTWOOD

RONALD REAGAN

MICK JAGGER

WINSTON CHURCHILL

RICHARD NIXON

FIG. 3.5. Caricatures of famous faces produced using the Caricature Generator.

A considerable amount of work on face recognition has been based on quite a different assumption, namely that a fixed set of features, some of which are more important than others (e.g. the eyes may be more important than the nose), are coded for all faces (for reviews see Rhodes, 1985; Shepherd, Davies, & Ellis, 1981). In fact, until the advent of research on caricature recognition, very little attention had been paid to the idea that what is important may vary from face to face and to the possibility that we code whatever is distinctive about a face.

PHOTOGRAPHIC CARICATURES

Phil Benson and David Perrett of St Andrews University have modified Brennan's algorithm to produce caricatures of photographic-quality images (Benson & Perrett, 1991a, 1991b; Benson, Perrett, & Davis, 1989) (see Fig. 3.6). As in Brennan's system, a face is represented as a set of points, each point is compared with the corresponding point on a norm face, and differences between these pairs are exaggerated or reduced by a specified amount to produce caricatures and anti-caricatures, respectively. Therefore, the degree of distortion is determined in exactly the same way as for a line drawing caricature.

However, to produce a photographic-quality caricature, the brightness variation across the surface of the original face must then be mapped into the distorted face. The mapping is done as follows. First, the face is divided into 340 triangle-shaped regions (tessellations) by joining triads of adjacent points and by joining points on the boundary

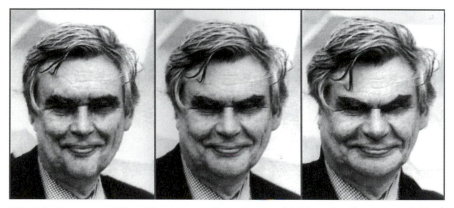

FIG. 3.6. Benson and Perrett's photographic caricature (right) and anticaricature (left) of the psychologist Richard Gregory. The undistorted photograph appears in the centre. Reprinted from *Perception*, 1991, *20*, p.279, with permission from Pion Ltd., London. (Photograph: Phil Benson.)

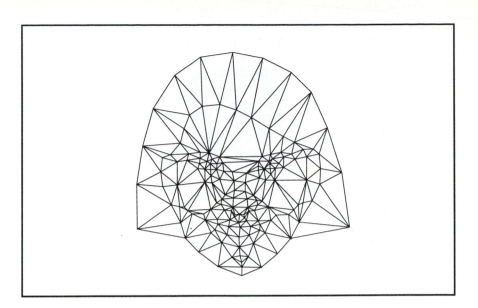

FIG. 3.7. The tessellations used to create photographic caricatures. Of the 340 tessellations, 42 link the edge of the head with the picture frame. These are not shown. (Photograph: Phil Benson.)

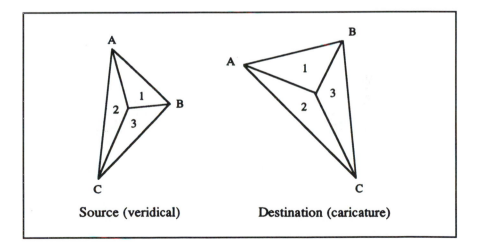

FIG. 3.8. The triangles used to map grey levels from the undistorted image to the caricature (or anticaricature). (Photograph: Phil Benson.)

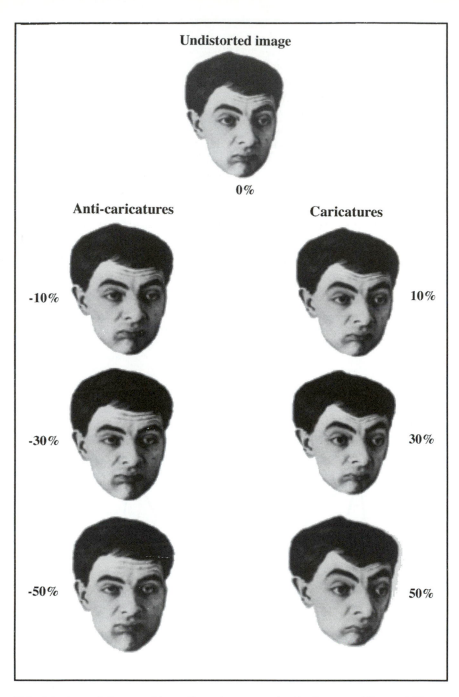

Undistorted image

0%

Anti-caricatures   **Caricatures**

-10%   10%

-30%   30%

-50%   50%

FIG. 3.9. A set of photographic-quality caricatures and anticaricatures of Rowan Atkinson.

with those marking the internal hairline (Fig. 3.7). Second, a corresponding set of tessellations is created on the distorted face, so that the two images can be compared. Third, each tessellation is divided into three triangles with a common vertex defining the centroid of the tessellation (Fig. 3.8). Finally, the grey levels are mapped from the original tessellations into the new distorted ones, by stretching or shrinking the distribution of pixels along radial lines traversed from each pixel on the outer edge to the centroid. The result is a photographic caricature.

Commercial packages have recently become available that can create photographic caricatures, so that the scope for merciless manipulation of friend and foe is limited only by your imagination! These packages should also provide researchers with more realistic stimuli than the line drawings that have been employed in many caricature recognition studies. A set of photographic-quality caricatures produced using the package Morph is shown in Fig. 3.9.

CHAPTER FOUR

Peacocks' tails and other natural caricatures

In species after species, particularly among birds and insects, the females are economically and sensibly dressed, obeying Darwinian dictates, whereas the males flagrantly flout the rules, flying in the face of natural selection and going in for gaudy colors, baroque ornamentation or elaborate song and dance routines. The peahen could have been designed by a hard-headed cost-cutting engineer; her mate could have stepped off the set of a Hollywood musical.

Cronin (1991) p.113

Before I turn to psychologists' efforts to understand the power of caricatures, I want to consider the case of natural caricatures. Like human artists, animals also exploit the power of caricatures. Extravagant sexual ornaments like the peacock's gaudy tail, the baroque splendour of bird of paradise tails, the mannerist tails of lyrebirds, widowbirds, and swallows, and the nightingale's complex song are all caricatures or exaggerations of standard-issue attributes. Extreme signals are also used outside of the courtship arena. Elaborate song and fancy plumage deter rivals, brilliant coloration and extreme movements deter predators, and the conspicuous and exaggerated begging signals of young birds elicit feeding (for a review see Zahavi, 1991). In this chapter I will investigate why these natural caricatures are so common and what they tell us about the nature of recognition systems. I will begin, as biologists have done, with the case of extravagant sexual ornaments (for more detailed discussions see Andersson, 1994; Cronin, 1991; Gould & Gould, 1989; Ridley, 1993).

NATURAL CARICATURES: FEMALE PREFERENCES AND SEXUAL SELECTION

Extravagant sexual ornaments have fascinated biologists since Darwin, not simply because of their visual appeal, but because they pose a problem for Darwin's theory of natural selection. If, as the theory proposes, traits are selected by virtue of their survival value, how then can such profoundly non-utilitarian traits have arisen? At best, extreme sexual ornaments are impractical and at worst they seriously impede survival. Long tails hamper mobility and conspicuous colours, songs, and displays attract predators as well as potential mates. Darwin struggled with this puzzle, confessing that, "The sight of a feather in a peacock's tail, whenever I gaze at it, makes me sick!" (Darwin, 1887, p.296).

To resolve the paradox of natural caricatures Darwin appealed to the aesthetic sensibilities of females. He proposed that males with extreme traits benefit reproductively simply because females prefer to mate with them. This process of *sexual selection* explains how natural caricatures could evolve, despite there being little *direct* survival benefit, or even a cost, to the trait. The reproductive edge conferred by female preferences would offset any direct survival costs.

Many of these extreme traits appear beautiful to us, and may even be plundered for use in human adornment (see Fig. 4.1). But do female animals really have aesthetic preferences? Darwin's claim that they do provoked a lively 19th century debate, with many of his contemporaries, including the co-discoverer of natural selection, Alfred Russel Wallace, rejecting the idea as absurd (Cronin, 1991).

Contemporary scientists are less sceptical about aesthetic preferences in animals because, unlike the Victorians, they don't equate preferences with *conscious* aesthetic judgments or even necessarily with cognitive processing (Kirkpatrick & Ryan, 1991)[1]. Rather, they have approached Darwin's proposal with an open mind, asking whether or not animals have the right sort of preferences to account for the evolution of natural caricatures and whether the preferred males actually have enhanced reproductive success. Their findings support Darwin's conjecture, with females preferring extreme or exaggerated sexual ornaments and displays over more modest ones, and the

FIG. 4.1. Avian sexual ornaments used for human adornment: Tribesmen from Papua New Guinea adorn themselves with bird of paradise feathers. Similar examples can be found in many cultures. (Photograph: Susan Allard.)

preferred males indeed enjoying a reproductive advantage (for reviews see Harvey & Bradbury, 1991; Ryan, 1990; Ryan & Keddy-Hector, 1992). One recent review documents over 150 studies demonstrating extreme preferences by females (Ryan & Keddy-Hector, 1992).

A few examples will illustrate the typical findings of these mate choice studies. One classic study featured male widowbirds *Euplectes progne*. These small birds sport tails over half a metre long, which render their flight displays visible for over a kilometre. Andersson (1982) asked whether females would prefer males with longer tails than normal, as required for the evolution of long tails. His cut and paste approach left nine birds with super-long tails, nine with super-short tails, nine with reglued tails of the original length, and nine with their original tails intact. The super-tail males ended up with more than twice as many new nests on their territories as any other males. Given that females nest on the territories of their mates, this result suggests that the females preferred the super-males. Female preferences are not the only way that super-tails can confer a reproductive advantage. Super-tails might also intimidate other males, with reproductive success resulting from male–male competition rather than female preferences. Andersson examined this possibility, but found that tail length had no effect on a male's success in holding a territory. Therefore, males with extra-long tails seem to enjoy a reproductive edge over their fellows because females prefer them.[2]

Male widowbirds are polygynous (one male mating with several females), and preferred males enjoy greater reproductive success because more females choose to mate with them. However, female preferences can also affect male fitness in monogamous species. Like the polygynous widowbirds, monogamous female swallows *Hirundo rustica* prefer males with extreme tail ornaments (Møller, 1988).[3] Long-tailed males find mates more quickly (see also Smith & Montgomerie, 1991) and produce significantly more fledglings than control birds (with tails cut and reglued or tails untouched) and birds with experimentally shortened tails. Long-tailed males are also more successful in their sneaky sexual advances to females other than their mate. Like Andersson, Møller also considered the possibility that male–male competition might contribute to the reproductive success of long-tailed males. He found that tail length was not related to territory size or mate guarding and so his results support Darwin's idea that female preferences affect male reproductive success.

Female preferences have also been found for extreme tail markings. When Hoglund, Eriksson, and Lindell (1990) enlarged the white tips on the male tail feathers of great snipe *Gallinago media*, control males with normal markings became spectacularly unpopular. Of the 17 observed matings, 16 were to males with enlarged white spots.[4] Peahens show a similar preference for extreme tail markings, shopping around for the peacock with the most eye-spots (Petrie, Halliday, & Sanders, 1991).

Female preferences may even extend to a male's "assets", with female satin bowerbirds *Ptilonorhynchus violaceus*, choosing males based on the quality of their bowers (Borgia, 1986). Thus the mating success of male bowerbirds is strongly and positively correlated with the elaborateness of their bowers. When Borgia removed decorations from bowers, willing mates dwindled along with the decorations. Male birds also exploit this effect, often completely destroying their competitors' bowers. Although Borgia did not enhance any bowers, it seems very likely that enhanced bowers would enhance mating success.

All of the preferences for extreme traits discussed so far have been shown by female birds. However, such preferences are common in the mate choices of many species. Ryan (1990) reviews cases of extreme preferences in frogs (for lower-frequency calls, calls with more notes, faster call rates, more calls, and more intense calls), toads (for high call rates), crickets (longer calling bouts), fish (longer tails, larger body size, larger areas of bright colour), newts (males prefer stronger female pheromones), butterflies (males prefer females with larger wings and faster wing beats), and moths (larger body size, more pheromone). Many of these preferences are for extremes that fall within the natural range of population variation, but when exaggerated stimuli outside of this range have been included, they are generally preferred (Andersson, 1982; Magnus, 1958, cited in Ryan, 1990; Rowland, 1989a,b; Sullivan, 1983)[5].

FEMALE CHOICE: AESTHETICS OR ASTUTENESS?

Some females certainly show the preferences needed for Darwin's account to work and the preferred males have a reproductive edge over their rivals. Thus sexual selection and the existence of female choice are now well accepted. There is still a vigorous debate, however, about exactly how female choice operates in sexual selection. Darwin was vague about this issue, and it was not until 50 years later that Ronald Fisher proposed a mechanism (1915, 1930).

Fisher's idea was that female preference for a male trait would cause both the trait and the preference to spread in the population, because male offspring will have the desirable trait and female offspring will have the preference.[6] The males benefit because they are preferred and the females with the preference benefit because their sons are preferred. The result is a feedforward or *runaway* process in which both the trait and the preference spread in the population. Extravagant male ornaments, such as peacocks' tails, will evolve so long as the female preference is a *relative* one (e.g. for the longest tail on offer) rather than an absolute one (e.g. for tails of a certain length—unless that length was way beyond the current maximum). Escalation will occur until checked by some opposing process. At some point, for example, increased costs associated with an extreme trait may eliminate the net fitness advantage conferred by sexual selection.

Neither Fisher nor Darwin supposed that the preferred males were inherently superior to other males. Darwin's contemporary, Wallace, offered a radically different proposal, suggesting that females with extreme preferences might actually be choosing the healthiest males and directly enhancing their own reproductive success (Wallace, 1889, 1891). They may be showing *good sense* rather than *good taste*, making astute choices rather than purely aesthetic ones. Wallace defended his proposal with the observation that bright plumage and elaborate displays often reflect good health and a robust constitution. Thus by choosing males with extreme versions of these traits the females would be choosing the healthiest males.

More recent research supports this link between health and appearance. In a classic paper Hamilton and Zuk (1982) reasoned that if females are using sexual ornamentation to choose the least parasitised males, then species that suffer most from parasite infections should be the most likely to have evolved extravagant ornaments. In a less parasitised species there would be less selection pressure for such good-health indicators. This prediction was supported by their analysis of over 100 species of songbird. By choosing males with the most extreme traits, females choose the healthiest male and gain two benefits. They reduce the risk of infection to themselves and their offspring, and they probably mate with a genetically superior male. Although there is some debate about the validity of Hamilton and Zuk's cross-species comparisons (see Kirkpartrick & Ryan, 1991), their conclusions are supported by studies showing that the quality of sexual ornamentation reflects male health (Møller, 1990; Wedekind, 1992).

Recent evidence that attractive tail ornamentation indicates genetic quality also supports Wallace's "good sense" hypothesis. Petrie (1994) found that the offspring of peacocks with the most elaborate tails grow better and are more likely to survive than the offspring of less well endowed males. This was the case even though females were mated with random males and the offspring were reared under identical conditions. Therefore, tail ornamentation appears to indicate genetic quality, making it sensible for peahens to choose the male with the most elaborate tail.

Extreme traits are not the only signals of male quality that are attractive. Symmetry, which is easily disrupted by environmental and genetic stress (Palmer & Strobeck, 1986; Parsons, 1990; Thornhill & Gangestad, 1994), is also attractive (Brooks & Pomiankowski, 1994; Concar, 1995; Møller, 1992; Møller & Pomiankowski, 1993; Thornhill, 1992; Thornhill & Gangestad, 1994; Watson & Thornhill, 1994). In one study, Møller (1992) manipulated symmetry by lengthening or shortening the outermost tail feathers of barn swallows *Hirundo rustica*. The males with more symmetric tails found mates more quickly and had more fledglings than less symmetric males. Symmetry had no direct effect on male–male competition or offspring quality, suggesting that female preference was responsible for the differences in reproductive success. Female scorpion flies also prefer the scent of males with more symmetric wings (Thornhill, 1992). Finally, symmetry appeals to humans (Concar, 1995; Thornhill & Gangestad, 1994). Individuals with more symmetric bodies reported more sexual partners than those with less symmetric bodies. More symmetric males, but not females, also reported having their first sexual intercourse at a younger age than their less symmetric fellows (Thornhill & Gangestad, 1994).

Returning to natural caricatures, Wallace recognised that elaborate traits could be costly to their owners, but he considered them to be minor inconveniences rather than serious handicaps. More recent versions of the "good sense/genes" idea, however, have assigned these costs a crucial role in sexual selection and the evolution of natural caricatures. According to Zahavi's (1975) *handicap principle*, it is precisely *because* the handicaps are substantial that they are effective advertisements for a male's (genetic) quality. They are a form of bragging, effectively saying, "look how well I can cope despite dragging this ridiculous tail around". Therefore, a preference for elaborate traits ensures that females are choosing the best males. Møller's symmetry study, described earlier, suggested that long tails can be a handicap, because natural tail length and symmetry were positively correlated. Given that deviations from the norm are usually associated with greater asymmetry, the positive correlation is a strong hint that tail length may be functioning as a handicap that can only be tolerated by the best swallows (Ridley, 1992).

Both good genes and good taste accounts have some plausibility. Modelling studies have demonstrated that both can both work in principle (for reviews see Bradbury & Andersson, 1987; Harvey & Bradbury, 1991). Moreover, the co-occurrence of genes for female choice and for exaggerated male sexual ornaments, required by these co-evolutionary accounts, seems to exist, at least in stalk-eyed flies, guppies, and sticklebacks (Pomiankowski & Sheridan, 1994).

So who was right, Darwin or Wallace? Recent studies suggest that *both* were right. Both "good genes" and "good taste" have probably contributed to the evolution of natural caricatures. Balmford, Thomas, and Jones (1993) have shown how each process may have contributed to different instances of an extreme trait like a long tail. They demonstrated that the aerodynamic costs of lengthening a tail depends on the shape of the tail, so that different kinds of long tails probably evolved differently. For example, lengthening graduated tails rapidly incurs aerodynamic costs (see Fig. 4.2) so that such tails could well have evolved as reliable indicators of mate quality via a handicap process. However, the same process is unlikely to account for the development of long streamer-shaped tails (pin tails and deep forks), which have much smaller marginal costs. Balmford and his colleagues suggest that the initial evolution of streamers is more likely to be the result of a Fisherian runaway process, especially for non-migratory families in whom flight is relatively unimportant. Finally, their analysis showed that, contrary to popular assumption, long tails need not always be costly. For example, initial lengthening of tails with a shallow fork actually benefits flight. Therefore, the development of these tails might

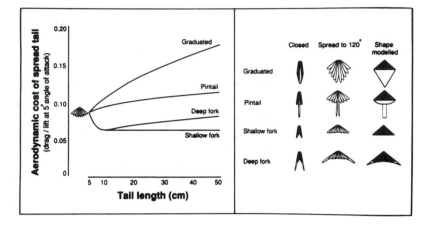

FIG. 4.2. Aerodynamic costs associated with lengthening of different types of tail. Reproduced from Balmford et al., (1993) with permission.

occur via direct selection with no contribution from sexual selection at all, or by some combination of sexual and direct selection.

Balmford and his colleagues have shown how different mechanisms can underlie the development of extreme traits, even different instances of the same trait. Some may be selected for because they function as handicaps that signal genetic quality, others may simply be preferred, and still others may actually confer a direct advantage. Presumably different selection pressures may also operate on the same trait at different points in its evolutionary history. Møller and Pomiankowski (1993) reinforce the point that different mechanisms can operate for the same kind of trait in different circumstances. They found a positive correlation between length and symmetry for peacocks' tails, widowbirds' tails, and beetle horns, consistent with the idea that long tails are functioning as a handicap. However, for pheasants and quetzals, they found the opposite association, with larger feathers being less symmetric than smaller feathers, suggesting that their long tails are not operating as a handicap. It will be very interesting to see if the kind of cost analyses carried out by Balmford and his colleagues could predict the patterns of association found for these and other pairs of traits.

PREFERENCES AND PERCEIVER PSYCHOLOGY

There is no doubt that female preferences for extremes play an important role in the evolution of extravagant sexual ornaments and displays in males, but why do females have such preferences? Darwin himself did not even raise this question, at least not explicitly (Cronin, 1991), but some years later Fisher (1915, pp.184–185) asked:

> Whence ... has this extremely uniform and definite taste for a particular detailed design of form and color arisen? Granted that while this taste and preference prevails among the females of the species, the males will grow more and more elaborate and beautiful tail feathers, the question must be answered 'Why have the females this taste?'

We have seen that part of the answer is that female preferences can be maintained in a population through sexual selection (via Fisherian runaway or good genes mechanisms). But this does not answer the deeper question of where the preferences come from *in the first place*. Almost 80 years after Fisher posed the question an answer is forthcoming. A consensus is emerging that many of these preferences simply reflect the way that sensory, perceptual, or cognitive systems work (Basolo, 1990a; Eberhard, 1990; Guilford & Dawkins, 1993; Kirkpatrick & Ryan, 1991; Pagel, 1993; Ryan, 1990; Ryan, Fox, Wilczynski, & Rand, 1990; Ryan & Keddy-Hector, 1992; Ryan & Rand, 1990, 1993; Searcy, 1992; Shaw, 1995; Small, 1992).

For example, the "push-up" display of insectivorous lizards seems to capitalise on a visual specialisation for detecting the motion of prey, the chucks produced by some species of frog have a frequency range that dovetails nicely with the tuning of the frog's auditory system, and the proliferation of eye-spots on the peacock's tail may capitalise on the attention-grabbing properties of eyes generally. In these and many other cases the details of the preferences seem to match idiosyncratic specialisations of a species' perceptual apparatus (see Kirkpatrick & Ryan, 1991 for other examples).

The idea that preferences reflect the psychological landscape of the perceiver explains both the incredible diversity of male sexual ornaments and the consistent female preference for extremes. The diversity of male traits stems from the variety of sensory, perceptual, and/or cognitive specialisations that they exploit in different species. The consistent preference for extremes reflects a more general feature of perceptual systems, namely that extreme signals elicit stronger responses.[7] Extreme signals are more noticeable, more discriminable, and/or more memorable than less distinctive ones. For example, perceptual systems respond more strongly to stronger than to weaker signals (Sekuler & Blake, 1990). Therefore, females who prefer more conspicuous males will spend less time searching for a mate, so minimising the chance of predation and the loss of foraging time. A preference for extreme versions of features that are relevant to mate recognition may also reduce errors, such as attempts to mate with immature or heterospecific males.

The idea that, ultimately, female preferences reflect the psychology of the perceiver leads to an intriguing prediction—that the preferences might predate the preferred traits. This seems like a difficult prediction to test, but a few ingenious attempts have been made. Studies by Michael Ryan and his colleagues, examining the preference of female frogs for low frequency "chucks" in male calls, illustrate the approach (Kirkpatrick & Ryan, 1991; Ryan & Keddy-Hector, 1992). They examined four closely related species of *Physalaemus* frog and found that females of *P. coloradorum* preferred male calls with chucks, even though chucks do not occur in that species. Females of *P. pustulosus*, whose males do have chucks, also showed this preference. The pattern of relationship between these and two other closely related species suggested that the preference, but not the chucks, was present in the common ancestor of all four (see Fig. 4.3 for details). An alternative interpretation of these data is possible, namely that the common ancestor had both the preference and the chucks and that the chucks were lost in the two species that currently lack them. However, given that preferences for low-frequency signals exert clear selection pressure for the development of chucks and that there are no obvious selection pressures against chucks, Kirkpatrick and Ryan prefer the pre-existing bias interpretation. Similar phylogenetic analyses point to pre-existing biases for other features of frog calls as well (an amplitude modulated prefix and double calls) (Ryan & Rand, 1993).

Using the same logic, Alexandra Basolo (1990a) argued that a preference for swords, coloured extensions of the caudal fin, predates the emergence of swords in certain kinds of fish. Not surprisingly, swordtail females prefer males with longer swords (Basolo, 1990b). However, females of their close relatives, the swordless platyfish, also prefer males with (artificial) swords (Basolo, 1990a). Given that the common ancestor of the swordless platyfish and their sworded relatives was swordless, these results strongly suggest that the preference for swords came before the swords.

In these examples, the male trait seems to exploit some pre-existing bias in the female. Perhaps the clearest example of such sensory exploitation can be seen in male water mites who mimic the movements

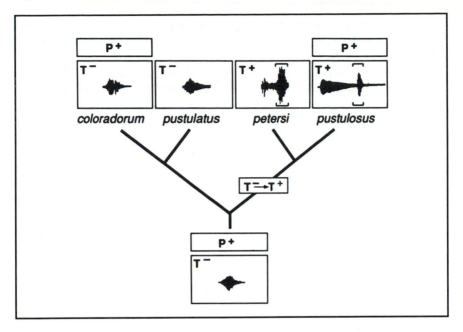

FIG. 4.3. Male display traits and female preferences in *Physalaemus* frogs. Only the closely related *P. pustulosus* and *P. petersi* add "chucks" to their calls (in square brackets) and so this evolved in their immediate ancestor. Females of both *P. pustulosis* and *P. coloradorum* prefer calls with chucks from which it is inferred that the common ancestor of all four species (bottom) had the preference. The preference for the chuck therefore evolved before the chuck itself did. (T -, no male chuck; T+, male chuck; P+, female preference for chuck. Oscillogram at bottom is typical of other calls in the genus). Reproduced (including caption) from Kirkpatrick and Ryan (1991) with permission.

of prey in order to attract females at mating time (Proctor, 1991, 1993). Hungry females on the look-out for a meal investigate and are mated more often than replete females! A phylogenetic analysis suggests that the hunting behaviour came before the courtship movements, consistent with the claim that the male display emerged to exploit a pre-existing bias.

Finally, in bird species where males use song as a display, females prefer males with larger repertoires (for a review see Searcy, 1992). Female common grackles, *Quiscalus quiscula*, also prefer males with larger song repertoires (combinations of songs from different individuals), despite the fact that these males have only a single song (Searcy, 1992). Therefore, large song repertoires, which resist the effects of habituation, may have evolved to exploit a pre-existing bias for variation or novelty, although in the absence of a phylogeny this conclusion must be regarded as tentative.

Evidence that a male trait appeared after the female preference gives perceiver psychology a *primary* role in the evolution of natural caricatures. However, some of this evidence has recently come under attack (Meyer, Morrissey, & Scharti, 1994; Pomiankowski, 1994). Basolo used a morphologically based phylogeny to infer a swordless common ancestor for swordtails and swordless platyfish, but a more sophisticated DNA-based phylogeny points to a sworded ancestor for the entire *Xiphophorus* genus (Meyer et al., 1994). Pomiankowski suggests that the new phylogeny, "invalidates the sensory exploitation hypothesis" (1994, p.494). But surely this conclusion is too strong. The new phylogeny does not rule out the possibility that the female bias predated swords. One simply cannot tell without going further back in evolutionary time. A new and apparently more accurate DNA-based phylogeny for the *Physalaemus* frogs has also complicated the interpretation of the chuck data (Ryan & Rand, 1993). Although the new phylogeny is consistent with a pre-existing preference, it is also consistent with a scenario in which preference and chucks evolved at the same time (see Pomiankowski, 1994 for details).

Despite these doubts about the phylogenetic evidence that female preferences actually predate extreme male traits, the hypothesis that those traits exploit the psychological landscape of the female remains an attractive one and will no doubt continue to receive close scrutiny.

The perceiver psychology hypothesis also predicts that preferences will not be limited to females. After all, the sensory, perceptual, and cognitive capacities of males and females are very similar. Although this prediction hasn't received much attention, a few studies have found male preferences for extremes. For example, male butterflies prefer extreme wing flicker rates (Magnus, 1958, cited by Marler & Hamilton, 1966), a preference that holds for rates well above those exhibited by real flying butterflies, and may be limited only by the ability to perceive high rates of flicker (Marler & Hamilton, 1966). Male threespine stickleback fish *Gasterosteus aculeatus* also show extreme preferences, preferring supernormal females with excessive abdominal distention or body size (Rowland, 1989b). Finally, male horned bees *Eucera nigrilabris* will try to copulate with flowers of the orchid *Ophrys tentredinifera*, which appear to be caricatures of the female horned bee (Barrett, 1987). These flowers seem to exploit the power of exaggeration to attract male bees as pollinators.

If males share the preferences of their female conspecifics, some of which result in the development of extreme sexual ornaments in males, then why are females so dowdy? A likely possibility is that the male preferences are not normally expressed because males generally aren't choosy (Trivers, 1972). Therefore, their preferences would have no reproductive consequences and so would not exert selection pressure for the development of fancy female sexual ornaments. If this possibility is correct, though, there ought to be fancy females in mating systems where males choose (e.g. polyandry). The wader *Phalaropus lobatus* is one of the few animals with this type of system and, as predicted, the usual plumage dimorphism is reversed. The females are brightly coloured and the males are dull (Halliday, 1978). One might also expect to find extreme female traits in monogamous species, such as humans, where males exercise some choice.

PERCEIVER PSYCHOLOGY, SIGNAL DESIGN, AND SUPERNORMALITY

I have argued that the extravagant sexual ornaments used to attract mates exploit a psychological landscape that favours extremes. However, this feature of perceiver psychology also provides an account of extreme signals that are not sexy. *Any* kind of signal could exploit a preference for extremes. Eye-catching, easily discriminable, and/or easily remembered signals will be more successful than those with little impact on their potential audience and animals would do well to use signals that exploit this aspect of perceiver psychology[8] (Endler, 1992; Guilford & Dawkins, 1991, 1993; Krebs, 1991). As Guilford and Dawkins (1991, p.3) put it so graphically, the perceiver's brain provides, "a complex psychological landscape across which messages must pass and to which signals have had to evolve". Perceiver psychology therefore offers an attractive hypothesis about the evolution of extreme signals in general, not just extravagant sexual ornaments.

In addition to exploiting the "complex psychological landscape" of the perceiver, extravagant characters may also make good signals because they are costly (Zahavi, 1991). Their costliness makes them difficult or at least "expensive" to fake. As a result, extreme signals tend to be reliable signals. Thus, extravagant signals may be effective *both* because of their impact on the perceiver (e.g. they attract attention) *and* because they are costly and hence reliable (see Dawkins, 1993 for further discussion).

If extreme signals have evolved to exploit a "preference" that is a fundamental component of perceptual/cognitive systems, then such preferences (or, more broadly, enhanced responses to extreme signals) should be widespread, and indeed they are. Supernormal preferences occur for a diverse range of stimuli and in a wide variety of taxa.

The early ethologists were the first to realise that the natural stimulus is often not the most effective one. Instead, stimuli that exaggerate some critical property of the natural stimulus, such as its size, contrast, or number, often produce an enhanced response. Thus Niko Tinbergen was able to build a super-gull by exaggerating the characteristics to which chicks respond. This caricature elicited stronger responses from the chicks than a real gull. After some difficulty, he chose the term *supernormal*[9] to describe this phenomenon (Tinbergen, 1953, p.207):

> What should we call this phenomenon? At first we called it, thoughtlessly, "super-optimal stimulus"[10], a contradiction in terms, since "optimal" by definition cannot be exceeded. "Supernatural" would be a good term, if it were not used already in another sense. We have, therefore, chosen the term, "supernormal".

Supernormality intrigued Tinbergen, who believed that the phenomenon could be observed in humans as well as animals, offering lipstick and the exaggerated baby-features of Disney's *Bambi* animals as examples. Doll designers obviously share his views, creating super-baby and Barbie dolls.

In his classic work, *The study of instinct*, Tinbergen credits Koehler and Zagarus (cited in Tinbergen, 1951) with the discovery of supernormality. They noticed that ringed plovers prefer an egg with high-contrast black spots on a white background to their normal egg with dark brown spots on a light brown background. Once identified, numerous other supernormal effects were found. Tinbergen (1951) describes the comical attempts of oystercatchers to roll enormous eggs into their nests and to incubate super-clutches (see Fig. 4.4). Many other examples, including (mostly anecdotal) human ones such as super-baby faces, the exaggerated smiles of cartoons, and various styles of clothing and make-up, can be found in a review by Baerends (1982).

A preference for supernormal stimuli may also underlie the paradoxical nurturing responses of host birds to nest parasites such as cuckoos. New Zealand warblers, for example, feed cuckoo chicks despite the fact that they are not fooled by the chicks' attempts to imitate warbler begging calls (McLean & Rhodes, 1991; McLean & Waas, 1987). The extra-large gape of the over-sized cuckoo chick seems to act as a supernormal stimulus that overrides the discrepant auditory cues to elicit feeding behaviour from the adult warblers.

Supernormal stimuli are not restricted to the super-appealing. Super-aversive stimuli can also be created by exaggerating properties

FIG. 4.4. Oystercatchers prefer super-large clutches (above) and eggs (below). Reproduced from Tinbergen, N. (1951), *The study of instinct*. OUP, Clarendon Press, by permission of Oxford University Press.

that provoke fear. For example, the white wing markings of woodpigeons *Columba palumbus*, function as an alarm signal, and birds will avoid models with enlarged markings compared with those displaying normal wing marks (Inglis & Isaacson, 1984). Perhaps flying predators could also be made more frightening by exaggerating their short necks or overall body shape relative to that of non-predators.

The early ethologists focused on biologically important "sign" stimuli that trigger innate responses (e.g. feeding, nesting, mating). Later, behavioural ecologists generalised supernormality to other stimuli in adaptive contexts (e.g. O'Donald, 1977; Staddon, 1975; ten Cate & Bateson, 1988). The extravagant sexual ornaments, featured earlier in this chapter, can be thought of as supernormal versions of more modest earlier forms. People, as well as nature, have exploited the power of supernormal stimuli in a diverse range of contexts, from erotic art to fly fishing (Hammond, 1988).

CONCLUSIONS

Natural caricatures are common. In this chapter I have asked why this is so. The evidence suggests that many natural caricatures are a consequence of a psychological landscape that favours extreme signals. The peacock's tail and other extravagant sexual ornaments exploit this feature of perceptual systems. However, supernormal preferences are not restricted to these biologically significant stimuli. On the contrary, as we will see in the next chapter, supernormal effects occur for quite arbitrary stimuli. Extreme signals generally therefore may exploit a fundamental feature of recognition systems, namely their preference for extremes.

NOTES

1. Darwin himself had a more modern view of female preferences, noting that, "It is not probable that she consciously deliberates". (Darwin, 1871, ii, p.123)
2. Super-short tails are also extreme. However, the preference is for extremes that amplify an initially preferred deviation from the norm. In other words if an attractive trait is larger/brighter/fancier than normal, as in sexual ornaments, then the preference will be for extremes that exaggerate the deviation of those features from the norm. Alternatively, if the attractive trait was smaller/duller/plainer than normal, then the preferred extreme would exaggerate those features (super-small/dull/plain).
3. In Møller's study the elongated tails were actually at the upper limit of the normal range of tail length, so are not exaggerated. However, there is no reason to suppose that longer tails would not produce similar results.
4. Ten of these matings were to a single male, so it is possible that male–male competition might have contributed to these results (if that male happened to be a particularly capable individual). Also, he could have had some especially attractive feature(s) other than tail length, so that the result should probably be replicated before we can be confident that there is a genuine preference for exaggerated spots.
5. More complete discussions of sexual selection and mate choice can be found in numerous sources (e.g. Bateson, 1983; Bradbury & Andersson, 1987; Cronin, 1991; Halliday; 1978; Harvey & Bradbury, 1991).
6. On this view, female preference can be selected for, just as the male trait is selected for, and there is some evidence that this may be true. Female choice increases fitness for zebra finches *Poephila guttata* (Burley, 1986), seaweed flies *Coelopa frigida* (Crocker & Day, 1987; Engelhard, Foster, & Day, 1989), two-spot ladybirds *Adalia bipunctata* (Majerus, 1986), tungara frogs *Physalaemus pustulosus* (Ryan, 1983), and crickets *Gryllus bimaculatus* (Simmons, 1987). In the case of the ladybirds, the distribution of preferences in the offspring suggested that the female

preference was controlled by a single dominant gene, and although such a simple genetic mechanism is unlikely to underlie all female preferences, there is little doubt that female preferences can be selected for.

7. This view accounts for the *directionality* of selection pressure for more extreme and conspicuous traits, whereas a model like Fisher's runaway process has no inherent directionality and could account just as well for the evolution of less and less conspicuous traits.

8. Guilford and Dawkins (1991, 1993) use the term "receiver" psychology, to capture the notion of an organism as a receiver of signals.

9. Tinbergen did not, however, coin the term. The OED cites popular use in the nineteenth century with the meaning of exceeding what is normal (e.g. "this vast amount of super-normal celibacy").

10. *"Überoptimal"* occurs in print as early as 1942 (Tinbergen, Meeuse, Boerema & Varossieau, 1942, cited by Baerends, 1982).

CHAPTER FIVE

The power of extremes

*... It is an interesting thought that all nervous systems built
for recognition may share certain general biases which result
from hidden properties of the recognition system.*

Enquist and Arak (1993) p.447

In the last chapter we saw that supernormal effects are widespread in
nature and that many animal signals exploit a preference for extremes.
In this chapter I argue that the power of exaggeration may reflect an
intrinsic feature of recognition systems. Whenever stimuli or categories
must be distinguished, exemplars that exaggerate the differences
between those categories often elicit enhanced responses compared with
the learned exemplars. I turn now to the evidence that such a preference
for extremes is widespread, occurring in humans, other animals, and
even computer recognition systems.

PEAK SHIFT

One of the most consistent findings in the study of learning is that once
an animal has been trained to distinguish between a positive (rewarded)
and a negative (unrewarded) stimulus, an extreme version of the
positive stimulus will elicit a stronger response than the positive
stimulus itself (see Fig. 5.1). This shift in maximal responding to a

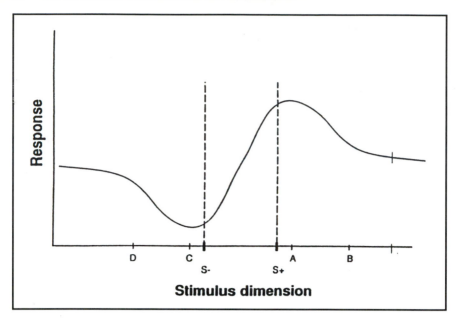

FIG. 5.1. The typical peak shift result. After training with S+ (rewarded) and S-(unrewarded), the strongest response is to a stimulus that differs more than S+ does from S-. Here the maximum response is shifted to point A. Note that the minimum response also shifts away from S-, in this case to point C. Reproduced from Weary, Guilford, and Wiseman (1993) with permission.

stimulus that exaggerates the difference between the rewarded and unrewarded stimuli is called *peak shift*, and it occurs for numerous recognition tasks with many kinds of animals, including humans (for reviews see Purtle, 1973; Thomas, Mood, Morrison, & Wiertelak, 1991).

To make the idea of peak shift more concrete, consider a typical discrimination learning experiment. A pigeon receives food from time to time (on a variable interval schedule) for pecking a key, but only when the key is illuminated by a green (550 nanometer) light and never when it is illuminated by a yellow (570nm) light. Eventually she will learn to peck the key when it is lit by the green light (S+) but not when it is lit by the yellow light (S-). Having learned this discrimination, the pigeon is then presented with a variety of wavelengths, ranging from 480nm to 620nm. How will she respond? In 1959 Harley Hanson asked this question and got a curious answer. Instead of responding best to the rewarded green light (550nm, S+), the peak response was to a 540nm light (also green) that was *further from* the unrewarded yellow light (570nm, S-) than the rewarded green light. This preference for the more extreme stimulus is the classic peak shift effect.

Peak shift can be thought of as a supernormal effect, with the strongest response to a stimulus that exaggerates the difference of a rewarded stimulus from contrasting unrewarded stimuli.[1] It has been demonstrated for a wide range of discriminations—of wavelength, size, line angle, auditory frequency or intensity, weight, numerosity, and so on—suggesting that preferences for extreme or exaggerated features are by no means limited to the selection of mates or other biologically significant discriminations. Rather, they seem to be a basic feature of generalisation performance whenever discriminations are made.

Most of the research on peak shift effects has examined discriminations within a single dimension. However, these effects may not be restricted to such simple discriminations. Perhaps the power of caricatures is a peak shift effect for more complex, multidimensional stimuli. Therefore, if we want to understand the power of caricatures, it may be useful to begin by considering the kind of mechanisms that could produce these simpler peak shift effects.

MECHANISMS UNDERLYING PEAK SHIFT

Researchers have assumed that a single mechanism is responsible for peak shift effects and have formed two camps, each supporting a different contender (see Thomas et al., 1991 for a recent review). In this section I will introduce the contenders and consider their merits.

The absolute model
The first contender wields the power of generalisation gradients. Its supporters claim that subjects in discrimination learning experiments learn to respond to *absolute* stimulus properties, like the actual wavelengths presented. For example, in the typical study described earlier, the pigeons would learn that green (550nm) is "good" (S+) and yellow (570nm) is "bad" (S-). The result is an excitatory generalisation gradient centred on green (550nm, S+) and an inhibitory gradient centred on yellow (570nm, S-). The response strength to any particular stimulus that the pigeon might encounter is then given by the *net* activation of excitation minus inhibition for that stimulus (Spence, 1937; see Fig. 5.2).[2] Therefore, the peak response may be to a shorter wavelength (e.g. 540nm) than the rewarded green light, because, although it receives less excitation than the green light, it may receive even less inhibition, resulting in higher net activation. The size of the peak shift will of course depend on the exact shape of the generalisation gradients associated with rewarded and unrewarded stimuli.

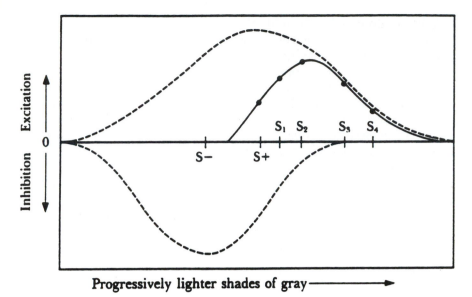

FIG. 5.2. An account of peak shift in terms of absolute stimulus properties. Excitatory and inhibitory generalisation gradients are centred on S+ and S-, respectively and response strength is determined by summing excitation and inhibition to give a net activation level (solid curve). After Spence (1937). Reproduced from Domjan and Burkhard (1986) with permission.

This "absolute" model predicts larger peak shifts when the rewarded and unrewarded stimuli are more similar and hence the overlap between excitatory and inhibitory forces is greater. This prediction is borne out in many animal studies, although it does not always occur with humans (for reviews see Purtle, 1973; Thomas et al., 1991). The model can even explain effects that seem to indicate that the animal is responding to the relationship between the rewarded and unrewarded stimuli, rather than to their absolute values. For example, an animal trained to respond to the lighter of two greys, may subsequently choose a lighter grey over the originally rewarded grey (e.g. Köhler, 1939). Spence interprets this "transposition" result in terms of the absolute model by proposing that the net excitation for the lightest grey is higher than for the rewarded grey because the former receives much less inhibition than the latter, being much further away from the unrewarded dark grey. Köhler himself rejected this absolute account of his transposition results, arguing instead that his animals had learned about the *relationship* "darker than". On this view the animal simply learns that when given a choice between two stimuli that differ in brightness it should respond to the lighter one.

Relational model(s)

The second contender for a mechanism that produces peak shift exploits just such *relational* stimulus properties (see Thomas, 1993 for a review). The idea is that, rather than learning absolute stimulus properties, the animal learns something about the relationship between the rewarded and unrewarded stimuli. Taking the wavelength discrimination experiment as an example, the pigeon might learn a simple comparative rule like, "shorter wavelengths are better than longer wavelengths".

The latest version of the relational mechanism is more sophisticated. The idea is that stimuli are compared to an adaptation level (AL), rather than directly to each other (Thomas, 1993; Thomas et al., 1991). This adaptation level should not be confused with evolutionary adaptation. In this context, "adaptation" refers to a calibration process by which perceptual systems adjust to the central tendency of inputs received (Helson, 1964). This central tendency defines the adaptation level to which stimuli are compared. The adaptation level is continually updated based on current and recent inputs, an effect that can be seen in some perceptual illusions. For example, in the waterfall illusion, prolonged exposure to downward motion resets the adaptation level so that downward motion becomes the reference point against which direction is judged and stationary displays appear to move upwards.

Applying this analysis to a typical peak shift experiment with two training stimuli, S+ and S-, we see that the adaptation level during training would be mid-way between the two (assuming that S+ and S- were presented equally often). If the rewarded stimulus is X units above this adaptation level, then the subject will learn the rule, "respond to AL + X", i.e. respond when the stimulus is X units above the AL. Now, suppose that the subject is tested with a set of generalisation stimuli centred on the rewarded stimulus (S+). This will result in a new AL of S+ and the peak response will now be to a stimulus X units above S+, producing the standard peak shift (see Fig. 5.3). Similar accounts can be given for other experimental situations. The crucial difference from "absolute" accounts is that the relationship between training and generalisation stimuli is central to the "relational" adaptation level account, but plays no role in "absolute" accounts. This difference also distinguishes the adaptation level account from earlier relational accounts (e.g. Gestalt accounts) that considered only the relationship between the training stimuli themselves.

The adaptation level account deals particularly well with human peak shift results (for a review see Thomas et al., 1991). For example, Thomas and his colleagues found that the peak shifted gradually over the course of generalisation testing, consistent with a gradual resetting of the adaptation level towards the centre of the generalisation series.

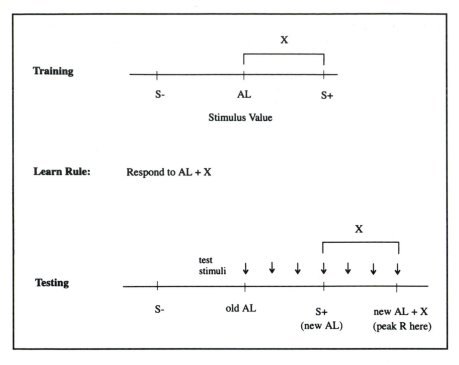

FIG. 5.3. An adaptation level (AL) account of peak shift. During training the AL is set midway between S+ and S-. If S+ is X units above this AL, then subjects learn to respond to a stimulus X units above the AL. During generalisation testing a new AL is set based on the range of test stimuli used. In the example illustrated the test stimuli are centred on S+, so that S+ becomes the new AL. Because subjects have learned to respond to a stimulus X units above the AL, peak response is to a stimulus X units above this new AL, i.e. X units above S+.

They were also able to increase the size of the shift by increasing the range of test stimuli on the side of the rewarded stimulus opposite to the unrewarded stimulus, as well as by increasing the separation of the rewarded and unrewarded stimuli (opposite to the prediction of absolute models).

Even more compelling support for the adaptation level view comes from Thomas et al.'s demonstration that peak responding can occur to stimuli on the *wrong* side of the unrewarded stimulus. They showed that subjects trained to respond to the dimmer (AL-X) of two stimuli (S+ dimmer than S-) had a peak reponse to a *brighter* stimulus than S- if the test set was centred on values brighter than S-. Such a test set results in a new adaptation level bright enough to make AL-X brighter than S-, causing the peak to shift to a stimulus on the wrong side of S-. Such a result cannot be explained by the absolute model. Nor can it be explained in terms of the relationship between the training stimuli alone. Only an adaptation level model seems able to handle this result.

Despite this impressive support for the adaptation level model, not all of the data are so easily accommodated. For example, Thomas et al. observed a double peak shift with two rewarded stimuli, one on either side of an unrewarded stimulus, and a test set that was symmetrically (and bimodally) distributed about the central unrewarded stimulus. The peak responses were to stimuli that were further from S- than the two S+ stimuli. Yet the adaptation level remained at S- throughout testing, so the peaks should *not* have shifted. Thomas and his colleagues tried to account for this double peak shift by suggesting that the value of X (the rewarded deviation from AL) also changes during generalisation testing. Their idea is that subjects may learn the rule, "respond to *slightly brighter* stimuli than S+" where *slightly brighter* is interpreted in the context of the range of test values. If this account is correct then the size of the double peak shift should increase with the range of test values, a prediction that was supported by the results of an additional experiment.

Thomas et al. present an impressive case for the relational, adaptation level account of human peak shift performance. For animals, however, Spence's "absolute" account works pretty well and, in some cases, works better than adaptation level theory. For example, the fact that the size of the peak shift increases as the rewarded and unrewarded stimuli get closer, mentioned earlier (e.g. Hanson, 1959), is predicted by Spence's theory, but is at odds with adaptation level theory (e.g. Hanson, 1959). Recall that the opposite pattern was obtained with humans. Does this difference mean that humans code relations whereas other animals only code absolute values of stimuli? Probably not. People can certainly code absolute properties (especially if they are using language to categorise and label stimuli) and other animals sometimes produce effects indicating relational coding (see Thomas et al., 1991, for examples). However, humans may be more likely than other animals to code relational properties.

Perhaps the most interesting implication of these studies is that absolute coding and relational coding can both generate a preference for extremes. If the stimuli are coded as absolute values on some dimension, then exaggeration can facilitate recognition if an extreme stimulus receives less inhibition and hence stronger net activation than the originally rewarded stimulus. More generally, an extreme stimulus may be less confusable with the unrewarded stimulus than is the rewarded stimulus. If the stimuli are coded in relation to an adaptation level or norm, then exaggeration can also enhance recognition. In this case, peak shift will be observed if the adaptation level changes so that an extreme stimulus has the same relationship to the new adaptation level as the rewarded stimulus had to the original adaptation level. If the adaptation level does not change then peak shift may still occur, although the explanation in this case is rather ad hoc, requiring that the size of the learned deviation (X) be adjusted to reflect the range of stimuli experienced.

CONNECTIONIST RECOGNITION MODELS AND THE POWER OF EXTREMES

The peak shift results suggest that preferences for extremes may be a fundamental property of recognition systems. Powerful support for this view comes from recent studies showing that even simple connectionist recognition networks display supernormal preferences (Arak & Enquist, 1993; Enquist & Arak, 1993; Tanaka, 1990; Tanaka & Simon, in press). In these networks, objects (inputs) are represented as patterns of activation across a set of interconnected units. The network can be trained to recognise a set of objects by adjusting the connection weights between the units so that the network gives the appropriate response (represented as patterns of activation in the outputs units) to each one. These networks are also known as neural nets, because the units can be thought of as neurons, with the connection weights indicating the strength of the link between each pair in the network. A detailed account of how such networks operate and their applications can be found in two volumes by David Rumelhart, James McClelland, and their research group (McClelland, Rumelhart & the PDP Research Group, 1986; Rumelhart, McClelland & the PDP Research Group, 1986).

If, as I have been arguing, a preference for exaggerated stimuli is a very basic characteristic of recognition systems, then networks that have been trained to recognise a set of stimuli ought to show a similar preference. The results of studies carried out by zoologists interested in explaining the evolution of natural caricatures (Arak & Enquist, 1993; Enquist & Arak, 1993) and psychologists interested in the power of caricatures to facilitate recognition of faces (Tanaka, 1990; Tanaka & Simon, in press) suggest that they do.

Enquist and Arak (1993) trained simple neural networks to recognise male conspecifics and found that the networks subsequently showed supernormal preferences. The architecture of the networks, each of which simulates a female bird who recognises conspecific males using simple visual cues, is shown in Fig. 5.4. The networks consisted of an input layer of 36 "retinal" units, a single output unit, and a hidden layer of 10 units. Each unit in the input layer connects to all the units in the

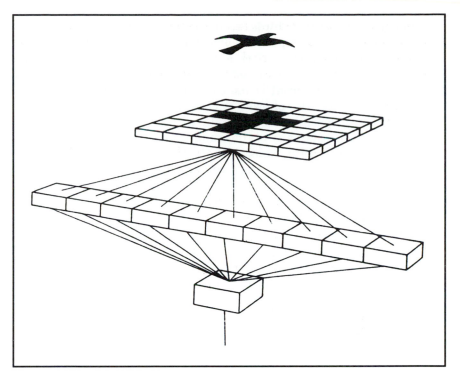

FIG. 5.4. The simple connectionist model used by Enquist and Arak (1993) consists of an input layer of 6 x 6 "retinal" units, 10 hidden units, and one output unit. Each unit is connected to all the units in the next layer (the connections for one receptor unit are shown). The network can learn to recognise a subset of training patterns (the output cell responds if it reaches a threshold of 0.5—for more details of the architecture see Enquist & Arak, 1993). Reproduced from Enquist and Arak (1993) with permission.

hidden layer and all the units in the hidden layer feed into the output unit. Stimuli (conspecific males) are represented as patterns of activation in the input layer and a recognition response is represented as activity in the output unit that exceeds a pre-set threshold level.

The training procedure mimicked the natural selection of recognition systems that occurs over evolutionary time. Beginning with a random set of connection weights, a new network was created by mutating some of the weights. (The probability of a weight being changed was 0.1 and when a mutation occurred the weight was increased by an amount selected randomly from a normal distribution with sigma varying from 0.1 to 0.4). The performance of the resulting network was compared with that of the old one and the better network was retained. This process was repeated until the probablility of an incorrect decision by the network was very low ($<10^{-5}$). The networks rapidly learned to discriminate long-tailed birds (conspecifics) from similar looking short-tailed birds (heterospecifics) and random images. Many different versions of the network, differing in the detailed pattern of their connection weights, were successful. These different versions can be thought of as using different visual cues to make the discrimination.

The trained networks showed a clear preference for exaggerated forms of the conspecific male. Inputs with extra-long tails elicited stronger responses than any of the training stimuli (see Fig. 5.5).[3] The converse also held, with weaker than normal responses to inputs without tails. Just as Andersson's widowbirds and Møller's swallows preferred extra-long tails, so too did the networks. Similar results were found for other networks trained to discriminate two kinds of "flower" (Arak & Enquist, 1993). Again, the trained networks showed supernormal responses to stimuli that exaggerated distinctive features of the "good" flower (as well as to other more arbitrary-looking patterns).

These networks simulate "learning" in an evolutionary timeframe. However, they can also be thought of as simulations of discrimination

Recognition task			Test images				
Reject	Accept		(a)	(b)	(c)	(d)	(e)
Random							
N: 20	16	48	32	16	24	60	16
I: 0.26	0.42	0.60	0.63 (66%)	0.68 (91%)	0.76 (100%)	0.34 (0%)	0.59 (50%)
II: 0.26	0.41	0.61	0.65 (74%)	0.68 (88%)	0.78 (100%)	0.35 (0%)	0.63 (57%)

FIG. 5.5. The network was trained to discriminate long-tailed birds (conspecifics) from short-tailed birds (heterospecifics) and random images, presented in various positions and orientations (N presentations per image). The average response (threshold = 0.5) is shown below each image for two trained networks (I and II). The networks show supernormal responses to images with longer tails (a, b) and wings (c) than the training image, as well as to some (uninterpretable) abstract patterns (e). In contrast they show particularly weak responses to images without tails (d). The figures in parentheses show the percentage of presentations of each image that elicited a higher response than the training image (conspecific). Reproduced from Enquist and Arak (1993) with permission.

learning in developmental time if the "selection" of networks following "mutation" is interpreted as reinforcement for correct responses. On this interpretation the behaviour of the networks suggests that supernormal preferences may be a fundamental feature of recognition/discrimination systems. Indeed Enquist and Arak acknowledge this interpretation when they suggest that some of the preferences exhibited are examples of peak shift.

Arak and Enquist regard these biases or "hidden preferences" of recognition systems as essentially non-adaptive. They see them simply as a consequence of the fact that many more possible stimuli exist than have shaped the evolution of recognition systems. As a result, recognition systems will inevitably have hidden preferences for stimuli that have never been experienced. However, a hidden preference for caricature-like stimuli, which exaggerate features that distinguish a target pattern from other familiar patterns, may well be adaptive because it minimises false positives, where a member of some other category is falsely recognised as the target. For example, supernormal preferences that reduced attempts to mate with a member of the wrong species, an immature conspecific, or a conspecific of the wrong sex, would be highly adaptive.

Arak and Enquist found supernormal preferences in networks with three layers—an input layer, an output layer, and a hidden layer. However, similar preferences can also be found in even simpler networks (Tanaka, 1990; Tanaka & Simon, in press). For example, Tanaka's (1990) network contained only an input layer, representing facial features, and an output layer, representing responses to different faces. The feature units could take on activation values of 0 or +1 and faces were represented by prototypical feature vectors. The vector (1,1,1,1,0,0,0,0) represented Joe, (1,1,0,0,1,1,0,0) represented Tom, and (1,0,1,0,1,0,1,0) represented Bob. Each of the eight feature units was connected directly to each of three face units. The network learned to recognise eight variations of each prototype vector. One feature was randomly changed from the prototype in each variation as a way of simulating the perturbations of a face produced by changes in expression or viewing conditions.

After training on these 24 exemplars, the network was tested with the three prototypes, a norm, and a 25% caricature of each face. The norm was created by averaging the feature values of the three prototypes, and the caricatures were created by increasing the difference of each feature value from the norm value for that feature by 25%. The prototypes produced higher activation than 23 of the 24 learned exemplar vectors, suggesting that the network had abstracted the prototype for each face (see Chapter 7 for a more detailed discussion of prototype abstraction). The caricatures for each face produced even higher activation. Not only was the activation of correct face units enhanced by the caricatures, but activity in the incorrect face units was suppressed. These results are consistent with the conjecture, proposed earlier, that a preference for extremes may increase the accuracy of recognition by reducing false identifications.

Although only a few studies have examined how connectionist recognition networks respond to caricatured or extreme stimuli, the results so far are quite consistent. In all cases, the networks showed a supernormal response to exaggerated stimuli, just like the peak shift response shown by natural recognition systems. Moreover, caricatures appear to inhibit incorrect responses as well as to facilitate correct responses. Taken together with the peak shift results, these modelling results suggest that a preference for exaggeration is a basic feature of recognition systems. Caricatures seem to enhance recognition performance in humans, other animals, and computers.

Another interesting feature of these connectionist networks is their preference for symmetry (Enquist & Arak, 1994; Johnstone, 1994). Enquist and Arak found that networks (similar to those described earlier) trained to recognise objects regardless of their position and orientation in the visual field preferred symmetric patterns.[4] Johnstone found that networks trained to recognise mates (i.e. to discriminate a set of four or five tail patterns from other patterns), showed not only the expected preference for extremes (longer tails), but also a preference for symmetric tails (compared with many other patterns). Symmetric patterns were preferred even when all the training patterns were asymmetric. Therefore, although a preference for symmetry may be adaptive because symmetry signals male quality, it may also be another intrinsic feature of a successful recognition system.

PEAK SHIFT, SUPERNORMALITY, AND THE DESIGN OF SIGNALS

The peak shift results have very interesting implications for the design of signals. They suggest that the best way to signal category membership may be to display exaggerated, rather than typical or average characteristics of the category, and we saw in the last chapter that this is precisely what happens in a variety of communication contexts. Therefore, at least some of the supernormal preferences exploited by these extreme signals may be the result of a peak shift effect (Hogan, Kruijt, & Frijlink, 1975; Weary et al., 1993).[5]

Take the case of extreme sexual ornaments. If females learn to discriminate conspecific males from females (and from males of other species), perhaps by sexual imprinting, then peak shift could result in preferences for exaggerated males.[6] As exaggerated males become more common, the exaggerated traits will become average, and peak shift effects will maintain a continued escalation. Thus the peak shift phenomenon during learning could produce female preferences that exert sexual selection pressure for extreme male traits. Ten Cate and Bateson (1988) have proposed a similar idea, suggesting that imprinting, combined with a bias towards slightly novel males (perhaps as a way of avoiding inbreeding), might account for extreme preferences. The peak shift results, however, suggest that the bias could emerge directly from discrimination learning during imprinting without any need for a separate process favouring novelty.

Weary et al. (1993) offer a qualification to these conjectures. They argue that because the amount of peak shift reduces as the stimuli to be discriminated become more distinct, peak shift effects could only produce modest amounts of sexual dimorphism. Therefore, although peak shift could produce an initial divergence, that modest dimorphism would have to be elaborated by other mechanisms of sexual selection. However, Thomas et al. (1991) showed that peak shift effects do not always get smaller as the rewarded and unrewarded stimuli become more distinct, so that peak shift effects may well be capable of generating substantial sexual dimorphism.

The traits that become extreme in males are ones that distinguish mature males from immature males and from females. Therefore, they are precisely the traits that should be exaggerated to facilitate mate recognition. Peak shift could therefore contribute to the evolution of elaborate sexual ornaments. Such ornaments could also signal male quality, because they require testosterone, which weakens the immune system, and so could operate as handicaps (Watson & Thornhill, 1994). Both factors would exert directional selection pressure on these traits. More detailed studies are needed to determine the relative contribution of these two factors to the evolution of natural caricatures.

The idea that peak shift effects can produce learned supernormal preferences is straightforward. A more speculative proposal is that innate supernormal preferences may also be the result of peak shift effects, but ones that operate in an evolutionary timeframe. For example, Staddon (1975) proposed that innate supernormal preferences might result when selection pressure is asymmetric, analogous to the asymmetry of reward in peak shift studies. As an example, he considers the preference for higher-than-normal flicker rates shown by some butterflies. If low flicker rates are commonly encountered and associated with avian predators, then there would be a considerable evolutionary cost associated with responding to them, but no corresponding cost for responding to high flicker frequencies. Perhaps such asymmetric evolutionary pressures result in an innate supernormal preference. Alternatively, innate supernormal preferences might simply reflect the design of effective recognition systems.

CONCLUSIONS

Exaggerated signals are highly effective for a variety of recognition systems. When humans, other animals, and connectionist networks must discriminate stimuli, or categories of stimuli, performance is often facilitated by exaggerating traits or features that distinguish the alternatives. This preference for extremes seems to be a fundamental feature of recognition systems, and one that imposes important constraints on the design of signals.

NOTES

1. An explicit contrast between the S+ and S- seems to be needed for peak shift to occur (Hogan, Kruijt, & Frijlink, 1975), but Terrace's (1966, 1968) stronger claim that S- must be aversive is controversial (see Honig & Urcuioli, 1981; Purtle, 1973).
2. In fact Spence predicted peak shift based on this reasoning before it was actually observed.
3. Enquist and Arak (1993) also showed that this supernormal preference could drive the evolution of longer tails and more extreme female preferences, when both tail length and the female recognition system were allowed to mutate. This was the case even with a survival cost for longer tails, although the degree of exaggeration became smaller as this cost increased.
4. During training, various mutations of the target pattern and of the network were tried, and the signal that elicited the strongest response and the network that discriminated best between the correct signal and others were retained. Ultimately a stable situation was reached with almost perfect performance by the network and little change in the signal. These stable signals tended to be symmetric, suggesting that symmetric objects are easier to recognise at a variety of positions and orientations in the visual field than are asymmetric objects.
5. Baerends and Kruijt (1973) warn against an uncritical accceptance of peak shift as the cause of supernormal preferences. The problem is that the specific learning conditions needed for peak shift may not be present in the natural situation. For example, it is not always clear what the unrewarded stimulus, S-, would be. Baerends and Kruijt illustrate this problem with a preference for super-large eggs. Eggs of another species

or objects other than eggs will not do as the unrewarded stimulus, because gulls don't try to retrieve them and so there is no opportunity for the response to extinguish (but this criticism rests on Terrace's controversial claims about the need for errors in training). Small gull eggs might constitute the unrewarded stimulus, with reward and non-reward (or punishment) corresponding to the number of offspring given large versus small eggs. This proposal could be tested by seeing whether inexperienced birds show the supernormal preference. More generally, the contribution of discrimination learning during development to supernormal preferences remains to be determined.

6.   Sexual imprinting may actually be a form of Pavlovian conditioning in which the imprinted object is both the conditioned stimulus and the unconditioned stimulus (Bolhuis, De Vos, & Kruijt, 1990; Suboski, 1990). However, peak shift occurs with Pavlovian as well as operant conditioning, so that the argument still holds (Weiss & Weissman, 1992).

CHAPTER SIX

The psychology of caricatures

The caricature may be faithful to those features of the man that distinguish him from all other men and thus may truly represent him in a higher sense of the term. It may correspond to him in the sense of being uniquely specific to him—more so than a projective drawing or photographic portrait would be ...

Gibson (1971) p.29

So far, I have considered the nature of caricatures, their development in the history of art, the invention of computer caricature generators, the use of extreme signals in nature, and some mechanisms that might account for the power of exaggeration. With this background in place, I turn now to cognitive psychologists' attempts to assess the effectiveness of caricatures and to discover whether caricatures really succeed in their paradoxical attempt, "to be more like the face than the face itself" (Brennan, 1985, p.170). Superportrait effects, where caricatures are recognised better than undistorted images, or are considered to be better likenesses, are the most dramatic evidence for the power of caricatures. Even equivalence of caricatures and more faithful representations would be remarkable, though, given the obvious distortion of caricatures.

INITIAL CLUES

Although the power of caricatures had been clear to artists and art theorists since the Renaissance, and although caricature-like peak shift effects had been observed in numerous discrimination learning studies, it was not until relatively recently that psychologists began to think specifically about caricatures and the effectiveness of exaggeration.

One of the first to do so was James J. Gibson (1947), who noticed that drawings from memory sometimes resembled caricatures. He made this observation during a study of methods for training airforce recruits to identify aircraft. The recruits were asked to draw, from memory, some of the aircraft they had learned to identify. The size of the images was constrained by marks indicating length and wingspan, so that Gibson could average the drawings of each plane made by different students and compare these with the originals (see Fig. 6.1). When he did so, he discovered that the averaged images consistently contained "*exaggerations* of those features of the shapes believed by the instructors to be characteristic and described by them in class. Some of the composites are even suggestive of *caricatures* of the planes" (Gibson, 1947, pp.136–137, my italics). Gibson speculated that the exaggerated features were ones that were important for differentiating the various memory images from one another, a notion supported by his finding that discrimination learning was better when these distinctive features, rather than the overall form, were emphasised during training. Thus features may not all be equal and which ones are important depends on the class of objects to be discriminated.

Gibson's study provides an important clue about how caricatures can be effective representations—they highlight those features that best distinguish each object from other similar objects. Eleanor Gibson (1969) also emphasised the importance of distinctive information in perceptual learning and object recognition, hypothesising that discrimination should be facilitated whenever distinctive features are enhanced: by maximising the number of possible feature contrasts, by eliminating non-distinctive features, or by exaggeration, as in a caricature. On this account, caricatures are effective because they tell you where in the image to find the important distinctive features. However, James Gibson's study raises an even more intriguing possibility. If drawings can be interpreted as externalisations of mental representations, then his results suggest that those representations might themselves be caricatured. If so, then caricatures would be effective because they match the memory representations better than undistorted images! I will return to this idea in the next chapter.

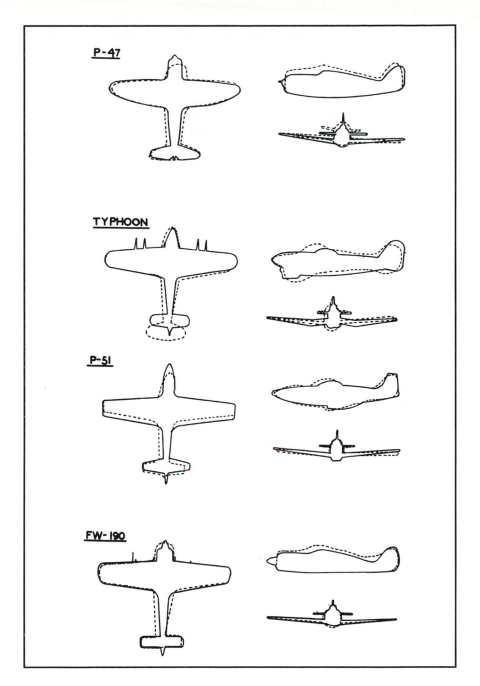

FIG. 6.1. Average shape of aircraft drawn from memory (dotted lines) superimposed on actual aircraft shapes. Reproduced from Gibson (1947).

A forerunner of experiments on caricature recognition was Ryan and Schwartz's (1956) study of how quickly structural details, other than outline shape, could be perceived in different kinds of pictures of known objects. They compared four kinds of pictures—cartoons, shaded line drawings, line drawings traced from photographs, and photographs. Although their cartoons probably don't show the systematic exaggeration of distinctive features that is the real hallmark of caricatures, they are simplified and "distorted ... to emphasise the essential spatial relationships involved" (1956, p.61) (see Fig. 6.2). Each subject saw either a hand, a switch, or a steam valve, shown in one of four possible positions, and was asked either to reproduce the hand position, name the switch that was open, or state the stage of the steam valve cycle shown. Exposure duration thresholds were determined for each task. Ryan and Schwartz did not statistically compare thresholds for the different kinds of image, but if we take differences exceeding 0.14 seconds (a difference that was significant at $p < 0.05$ in their comparison of the mean ranks of all four mean thresholds) to be reliable, then some interesting differences emerge. In particular, cartoons were at least as effective as the other kinds of pictures and were better than line drawings for hands and switches, and better than both shaded line drawings and photographs for switches. Therefore, to the extent that these cartoons are caricature-like, the results support the Gibsons' claim that caricatures should be effective stimuli, with a *superportrait effect* (caricatures better than undistorted representations) for some types of image and object and an *equivalence effect* (caricatures as good as undistorted representations) for others.

Another early study was inspired by the ethologists' discovery of supernormal stimuli described in Chapter 4. Gardner and Wallach (1965) asked whether supernormal stimuli could be created by exaggerating stimulus dimensions that trigger biologically significant responses. If they transformed the shape of a head to exaggerate "baby" features (large cranium, forehead, and eyes, fat cheeks, etc.), which elicit nurturing responses (Alley & Hildebrandt, 1988; Berry & Zebrowitz-McArthur, 1988; McCabe, 1988), would the head look more "babyish"? They created "super-babies" and "super-adults" (see Fig. 6.3), using parameters that gave minimal overlap between six adult male heads and six babies' heads, and found that the exaggerated baby heads were judged to be "more babyish" than the true baby head. Judgements of "more like a real baby" were also reported to increase with initial exaggeration and then decrease with further exaggeration, although the data were not presented. Overall, the results suggest a superportrait effect for the super-babies.

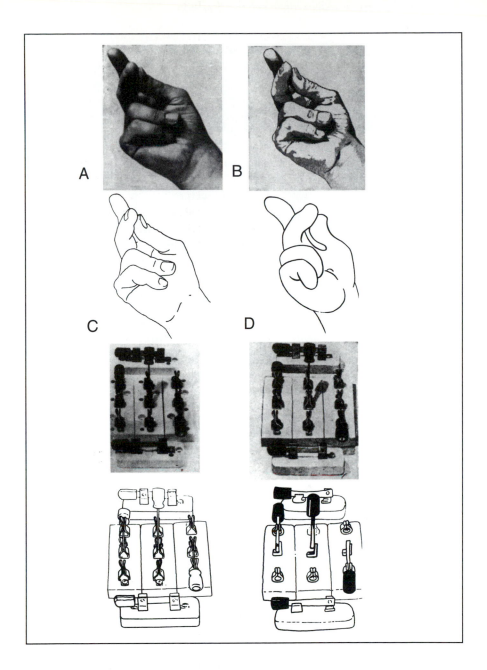

FIG. 6.2. Examples of the kind of images used by Ryan and Schwartz (1956): Photograph (A), shaded line drawing (B), line drawing (C), and cartoon (D) for a hand and a switch. Reproduced from Ryan and Schwartz (1956) with permission.

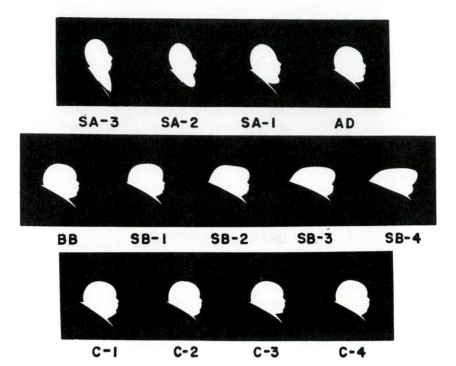

FIG. 6.3. The set of heads used by Gardner and Wallach (1965). SA = superadult, AD = adult, BB = baby, SB = superbaby, C = control. Superadult and superbaby faces exaggerate the difference between adult and baby faces, control faces contain a mix of baby and non-baby feature values. Reproduced with permission of authors and publisher from Gardner, B.T., & Wallach, L. Shapes of figures identified as a baby's head. *Perceptual and Motor Skills*, 1965, *20*, 135–142. © Southern Universities Press 1965.

Exaggeration of features associated with attractiveness in baby faces also produces a face that is preferred over more realistic faces (Sternglantz, Gray, & Murakami, 1977). The opposite pattern has also been observed, with the less babyish faces of preterm infants considered less attractive and eliciting fewer nurturing responses than normal baby faces (Maier, Holmes, Slaymaker & Reich, 1984). If it is not too fanciful to think of the faces in these two studies as caricatures and anticaricatures, respectively, then it appears that exaggeration facilitates, and de-exaggeration inhibits, the normal response to these faces.

The results of these studies suggest that caricatures can be potent stimuli. In all cases caricatures (or cartoons) were at least as good as undistorted images. In many cases they were better than undistorted images and they were never worse than the undistorted images.

Gibson's (1947) study of memory for aircraft silhouettes hints at the importance of distinctive features for recognition and raises the intriguing possibility that such features may be exaggerated in memory. Visual information also seems to be extracted at least as quickly from cartoons as from less distorted representations (Ryan & Schwartz, 1956). Gardner and Wallach's (1965) demonstration that supernormal stimuli enhance judgements of babyishness makes the crucial point that exaggeration can enhance the response normally associated with a stimulus. Therefore, it ought to be possible for a recognition response to be enhanced by caricatures. In the next section we will see that this is indeed the case.

LINE DRAWING CARICATURES

Brennan's computer Caricature Generator (1982, 1985), described in Chapter 3, offers researchers a powerful tool for creating stimuli to use in caricature recognition experiments. It allows direct control over the degree of distortion and the choice of norm against which to exaggerate a face. The direction of distortion can also be controlled, with the difference between a face and a norm increased to create a caricature, or reduced to create an anticaricature. Once an appropriate set of stimuli has been made, their effectiveness can be assessed by measuring recognition performance (speed and accuracy). If caricatures are superportraits, then they should be recognised more quickly and/or more accurately than "veridical", i.e. undistorted, images.

Recognition
Brennan's computer-generated caricatures were first used in a collaborative study, carried out at Stanford University, by Susan Brennan, Susan Carey, and myself (Rhodes, Brennan, & Carey, 1987). We took as our starting point the idea, suggested by the effectiveness of caricatures, that faces are mentally represented and recognised in terms of their distinctive features. If this is correct, then the effect of distorting a face should depend on how that distortion affects distinctive information. Specifically, a change that exaggerates distinctive information should be less disruptive to recognition than a change that reduces distinctive information, i.e. caricatures should be more recognisable than equally distorted anticaricatures. In addition to testing this *distinctiveness hypothesis*, we also tested the *superportrait hypothesis* (which we called the *caricature hypothesis*) namely that caricatures would be recognised better than veridical images.

We asked our subjects to name pictures of their colleagues, each seen as either a 50% caricature, an undistorted drawing, or a –50% anti-caricature. Male and female faces were caricatured against male and female norms, respectively. The caricatures were recognised four times faster (Mean = 3 seconds) than the anticaricatures (M = 12 seconds), supporting the distinctiveness hypothesis. They were also recognised twice as quickly (M = 3 seconds) as the veridicals (M = 6 seconds), supporting the superportrait hypothesis (see Fig. 6.4). Accuracy was quite poor (M = 33%), as in other studies using line drawings (e.g. Davies, Ellis, & Shepherd, 1978), and was not affected by caricature level. Interestingly, one of the subjects, a talented amateur artist who drew faces frequently and was much more accurate than the other subjects, showed a caricature advantage in accuracy, identifying all of the caricatures, 83% of the veridical drawings, and 50% of the anticaricatures. His results raise the possibility that caricature effects might also be found for accuracy if the images were more recognisable, a suggestion that has received support from subsequent studies (see later). Overall, the results indicate that distortion that highlights distinctive features facilitates recognition, whereas distortion that minimises those features disrupts recognition, consistent with our

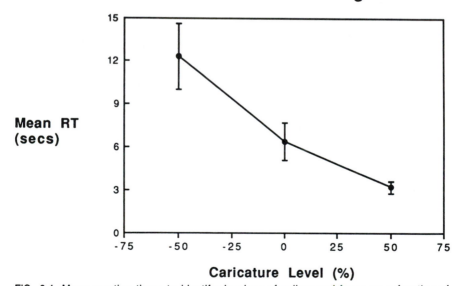

FIG. 6.4. Mean reaction times to identify drawings of colleagues' faces as a function of caricature level in Rhodes et al.'s (1987) study. Caricatures (50%) were identified twice as quickly as veridicals (0%) which, in turn, were identified twice as quickly as anticaricatures (-50%). SE bars are shown.

conjecture that each face is represented in terms of its distinctive features. They also show that caricatures can operate as superportraits, at least in the sense of being identified more quickly than undistorted images.

Further support for the superportrait hypothesis comes from a more recent study using enhanced line drawings (see Fig. 6.5) that are more recognisable than the plain drawings used in the previous study (Rhodes & Tremewan, 1994). The enhanced drawings had hair, irises and brows filled in, and glasses, moustaches, earrings, and any extra lines, not represented in the caricature program, added where appropriate. Impossible lines were also removed (e.g. where an ear comes inside the contour of the face or a wrinkle under the eye moves into the eye). Accuracy was much better than in the Stanford study, with nearly two thirds of the undistorted drawings recognised, compared with one third in the earlier study. Using a similar procedure to that study, but showing our subjects 10% and 30% as well as 50% caricatures, we found that high-school students recognised caricatures of their classmates better than undistorted images (see Fig. 6.6). On average 75% of the 30% and 50% caricatures were recognised, compared with 62% of the veridical drawings. These caricatures were recognised just as quickly as the veridicals.

Caricatures are also recognised more quickly and accurately than undistorted images when each face is shown at the caricature level chosen as the best likeness for that face (Benson & Perrett, 1994). Subjects selected the optimal caricature level for each face by adjusting the exaggeration level until they found the best likeness. On average, the best likeness was a 42% caricature in one experiment and a 54% caricature in a second experiment. Benson and Perrett then selected a subset of the most familiar faces in the second experiment (those with high optimal exaggeration levels) and compared recognition of these "optimal" caricatures with their undistorted counterparts. There was a clear caricature advantage for accuracy, with 64% of the caricatures recognised, compared with 50% of veridicals, and for speed, with caricatures taking about 3.8 seconds to recognise, compared with 6.0 seconds for veridicals. These times are remarkably similar to those reported by Rhodes et al. (1987) and the recognition rates are not dissimilar to those reported by Rhodes and Tremewan (1994).

These superportrait effects are not confined to computer-generated caricatures. Sarah Stevenage (1995a) has examined the effectiveness of artists' caricatures compared with undistorted drawings traced from photographs of famous faces. She found that people could name the caricatures more quickly (M = 865msec) than the undistorted drawings (M = 1012msec).

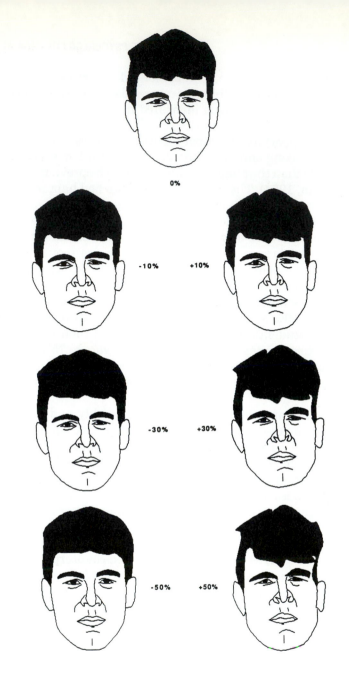

0%

-10%   +10%

-30%   +30%

-50%   +50%

FIG. 6.5. A set of enhanced line drawings used by Rhodes and Tremewan (1994). An undistorted face is shown at the top, with anticaricatures and caricatures at increasing levels of distortion in the left and right columns, respectively.

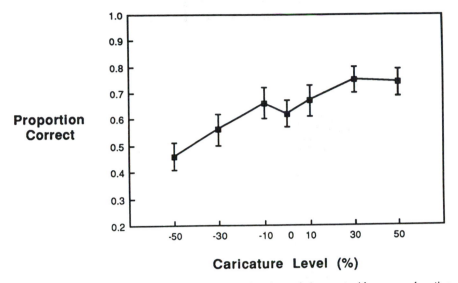

FIG. 6.6. Accuracy of identifying enhanced line drawings of classmates' faces as a function of caricature level in Rhodes and Tremewan's (1994) study. SE bars are shown.

A superportrait effect has also been found for relatively unfamiliar faces. Mauro and Kubovy (1992) showed their subjects a set of study faces and later asked them to indicate which faces in a test set (containing the study faces and new faces) they had seen before. They created caricatures using an Identikit system, giving each face a single distinctive feature (head height, nose height, or chin height) that was either exceptionally small or exceptionally large, and exaggerating these to produce caricatures. Other features were allowed to vary randomly. Mauro and Kubovy's subjects studied "faces" and "caricatures", which they subsequently had to pick out of a test set containing the study faces, study caricatures, (undistorted) faces of studied caricatures, caricatures of studied faces, and faces and caricatures that had not been seen previously. As predicted by the superportrait hypothesis, caricatures of previously seen faces were recognised better than the old faces themselves (at least for what Mauro and Kubovy call "true" caricatures, in which the exaggerated feature was distinctive in the original face).[1] Previously seen caricatures were also recognised better than previously seen faces, as would be expected given the greater distinctiveness of caricatures (Bartlett, Hurry, & Thorley, 1984; Cohen & Carr, 1975; Going & Read, 1974; Johnston & Ellis, 1995; Light, Kayra-Stuart, & Hollander, 1979; Valentine, 1991; Valentine & Bruce, 1986a,b).

A caricature advantage in a naming task suggests that caricatures access memory representations more effectively than undistorted images. However, the interpretation of a caricature advantage in the old/new task is less straightforward. It could occur because caricatures access memory representations better than undistorted images. But it could also occur because caricatures of *new* faces are more readily recognised as being new (giving a lower false alarm rate) than are new undistorted faces, due to the greater distinctiveness of caricatures. Nevertheless, Mauro and Kubovy's results are broadly consistent with the superportrait hypothesis.

The studies described so far have all used faces as stimuli. However, given the ubiquity of supernormal effects in nature and the power of exaggeration demonstrated by the peak shift results, it would be surprising if a caricature advantage was restricted to faces. So far, only one published study has examined caricature effects for other objects, but it gave similar results to the ones already discussed for faces. Rhodes and McLean (1990) examined bird identification and found that experts (professional ornithologists and keen amateur bird-watchers) identified 50% caricatures of passerine birds more quickly than undistorted drawings. Therefore, superportrait effects are not confined to face caricatures. As in the face studies, anticaricatures were recognised more slowly than either caricatures or undistorted images. The performance of non-experts was also examined, using a more heterogeneous set of birds (duck, goose, kiwi, pelican, etc.) that these subjects could identify. Although they did not show a caricature advantage, the non-experts recognised the caricatures just as well as the veridicals and recognised both better than anticaricatures. Whether the difference between these two groups of subjects is a genuine expertise effect or simply the result of using different sets of birds remains an open question. It may be that considerable experience with a class of stimuli is needed for a superportrait effect, or alternatively, it may simply be that more distinctive objects (e.g. the heterogeneous set of birds used for non-experts) benefit less from caricaturing than more homogeneous ones (e.g. passerines). In either case, caricatures of birds appear to be recognised at least as well as undistorted drawings, confirming that the power of caricatures is not unique to face recognition.

The results of the recognition studies discussed so far are summarised in Table 6.1. They show quite clearly that caricatures can function as superportraits. However, the most common finding is that caricatures and undistorted images are recognised equally well. For example, although Rhodes and Tremewan (1994—described earlier) found a superportrait effect for enhanced line drawing caricatures of one group of classmates' faces, they also found that caricatures and veridicals were identified equally well for plain drawings of those faces and for enhanced drawings of two other groups of classmates' faces and a set of famous faces. Caricature equivalence has also been found in a study by Lavin (1988) using profile silhouettes of colleagues' faces. This pattern also extends to non-face stimuli, with the non-expert subjects in Rhodes and McLean's (1990) experiments showing caricature equivalence for speed and accuracy to recognise birds.

Overall then, within the range of exaggeration that we have been considering (up to 50%), caricatures are at least as recognisable as undistorted images. Sometimes they function as superportraits, but more often they are recognised equally well as undistorted images. In only one study have these computer-generated caricatures been recognised more poorly than undistorted drawings (Rhodes & Moody, 1990) and that was for previously unfamiliar faces on which recognition performance (deciding whether or not the face had been seen before) was only barely above chance. Caricatures and undistorted images are also generally recognised better than anticaricatures, showing that metrically equal amounts of distortion have radically different effects depending on whether they exaggerate or reduce an object's distinctive features relative to a norm.

Likeness judgements

We have seen that caricatures are recognised at least as readily as undistorted drawings. Another way of assessing their effectiveness is simply to ask people how well a caricature captures a person's likeness. Would a caricature be considered a better likeness than an undistorted image? Or would people be reluctant to rate such obviously distorted (albeit readily recognisable) images as good likenesses, perhaps because they know that faces don't really look like that? Unlike anticaricatures and veridical drawings, which look like real faces, caricatures may contain impossible configurations with an eye rising above an eyebrow or the hairline above the top of the head. If caricatures are considered as good or better likenesses than undistorted images, despite such obvious anomalies, then their power would be considerable.

In the Stanford study (Rhodes et al., 1987) subjects were shown seven drawings of each person (-75%, -50%, -25%, 0%, 25%, 50%, 75%), told who they represented, and asked to rate how good a likeness each drawing was on a 7-point scale (1 = poor, 7 = great). The mean ratings for each caricature level are shown in Fig. 6.7.[2] Overall, the mean exaggeration level of the best likeness was 16%, which was significantly greater than 0%. However, this result does not necessarily mean that caricatures are superportraits, because 16% is an interpolated value, not a caricature level that subjects actually saw. Subjects *might* have

TABLE 6.1
Recognition of line drawing caricatures

Study	Stimuli	Dependent measure, Caricature levels used	Caricatures vs Veridicals*		
			Better	Equal	Worse
Rhodes et al. (1987)	faces (colleagues)	naming accuracy: Expt 1 −50, 0, 50		X	
		naming RT: Expt 1 −50, 0, 50	X		
Lavin (1988)	face profiles (colleagues)	name–face match: RT		X[a]	
Rhodes & Moody (1990)	faces (unfamiliar)	old/new: RT hits −50, −25, 0, 25, 50			X (50)
Rhodes & McLean (1990)	birds (non-expert Ss)	name–bird match: Expt 1 accuracy −25, −12.5, 0, 12.5, 25		X	
		name–bird match: Expt 1 RT −25, −12.5, 0, 12.5, 25		X	
	birds (non-expert Ss)	name–bird match: Expt 2 accuracy −50, −25, 0, 25, 50		X	
		name–bird match: Expt 2 RT −50, −25, 0, 25, 50		X	
		name–bird match: Expt 3 accuracy −50, −25, 0, 25, 50, 75		X	
	passerines (expert Ss)	name–bird match: Expt 3 RT −50, −25, 0, 25, 50, 75	X (50)		
Mauro & Kubovy (1992)	faces (unfamiliar)	sensitivity (old/new recognition)	X		
Benson & Perrett (1994)	faces (famous)	naming accuracy: Expt 2 optimal caricature, 0	X[b]		
		naming RT: Expt 2 optimal caricature, 0	X[b]		
Rhodes & Tremewan (1994)	faces (classmates A, famous)	naming accuracy: Expt 1 • all faces combined (plain & enh'd classmates A, plain & enh'd famous)	X (30,50)		
		• enhanced classmates −50, −30, −10, 0, 10, 30, 50		X	
		naming RT: Expt 1 • all faces combined		X[c]	
		• enhanced classmates A −50, −30, −10, 0, 10, 30, 50		X	
	faces (classmates B)	naming accuracy: Expt 2 • enhanced classmates B −30, 0, 30		X	
		naming RT: Expt 2 • enhanced classmates B −30, 0, 30	no main effect of caricature level		

Continued overleaf

TABLE 6.1 *(continued)*
Recognition of line drawing caricatures

Study	Stimuli	Dependent measure, Caricature levels used	Caricatures vs Veridicals*		
			Better	Equal	Worse
	faces (classmates A, C)	naming accuracy: Expt 3 • enhanced classmates A • enhanced classmates C −30, 0, 30		X X	
		naming RT: Expt 3 • enhanced classmates A • enhanced classmates C −30, 0, 30	no main effect of caricature level		
	faces (unfamiliar)	naming accuracy: Expt 3 • enhanced unfamiliar classmates A • enhanced unfamiliar classmates C −30, 0, 30	X	X	
		naming RT: Expt 3 • enhanced unfamiliar classmates A • enhanced unfamiliar classmates C −30, 0, 30	no main effect of caricature level		
Stevenage (1995a)	faces (famous)	naming RT	X		
TOTALS			**N = 8**	**N = 14**	**N = 1**

*Values in parentheses show which caricature level(s) (%) differ significantly from the undistorted image.
Equal means C = V and *both* better than A
[a] only for highly distinctive profiles
[b] no comparison with anticaricatures
[c] the only significant difference was that 50% caricatures were faster than −50% anticaricatures (0% did not differ from −50%)

99

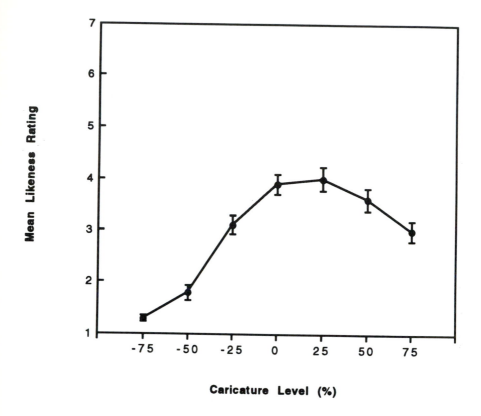

FIG. 6.7. Likeness ratings for drawings of colleagues' faces as a function of caricature level in Rhodes et al.'s (1987) study. SE bars are shown.

rated 16% caricatures as better likenesses than the veridicals if they had had the chance, but they did not have that chance. There was, however, clear support for caricature equivalence, with the 25% and 50% caricatures considered as good likenesses as the undistorted images. As in the recognition studies, distortion did not impair a likeness when it exaggerated distinctive information. In contrast, distortion that reduced distinctive information seriously degraded the likeness, with anti-caricatures considered significantly worse likenesses than veridicals for every caricature level tested.

Several other studies have found similar results, with caricatures consistently considered at least as good likenesses as veridicals. Table 6.2 summarises the results of these studies. In five cases the caricature level of the best likeness was significantly greater than 0%, and in two

TABLE 6.2
Likeness judgements for line drawing caricatures

Study	Stimuli	Caricature levels shown	Caricatures vs Veridicals[a]		
			Better	Equal	Worse
Rhodes et al. (1987)	faces (familiar)	Expt 1: −75, −50, −25, 0, 25, 50, 75	X (16)		
	faces (unfamiliar)	Expt 2: −25, 0, 25			X (na)
Rhodes (1993)	faces (famous)	−25, −12.5, 0, 12.5, 25	X (6)		
	birds	−25, −12.5, 0, 12.5, 25		X (−1)	
Benson & Perrett (1994)	faces (famous)	Expt 1: −50 → 250 … −150 → 150	X (42)*		
	faces (famous)	Expt 2: −50 → 250 … −150 → 150	X (54)*		
	faces (famous), internal features only	Expt 3: −50 → 250 … −150 → 150		X (5)	
Rhodes et al. (1996)	faces (famous, familiar)	−60, −50, … 50, 60	X (11)*		
TOTALS			**N = 5**	**N = 2**	**N = 1**

[a] Values in parentheses give the mean caricature level (%) of the best likeness.
Equal means C = V and *both* better than A
na = not available
* Caricature chosen as the best likeness

further studies it did not differ significantly from 0%. In only one study were caricatures considered poorer likenesses than undistorted images.

As already noted, however, an interpolated best likeness level significantly greater than 0% need not mean that caricatures are superportraits. A mean greater than 0% will result if caricatures and veridicals get equally good ratings, with anticaricatures receiving poorer ratings. So, do any of these studies show a genuine superportrait effect, with a caricature level that was actually presented chosen as the best likeness? They do. We have already seen that when Benson and Perrett (1994) gave their subjects control over the caricature level displayed, they chose 42% caricatures on average as the best likenesses for line drawings of famous faces. This superportrait effect was replicated in a second study in which 54% caricatures were chosen as optimal. Curiously, the caricature advantage disappeared when the same faces were shown without hair. A less dramatic, but nevertheless significant, caricature advantage was also found by Rhodes, Byatt, Tremewan, & Kennedy (1996), with 10% caricatures chosen most often as the best likeness from levels ranging from -60% anticaricatures to 60% caricatures in 10% steps, and a mean caricature level of 11% for the best likeness.

I suggested earlier that people might be reluctant to select obviously distorted images as good likenesses. If this conjecture is correct, then less extreme caricatures might be optimal for best likeness choices than for recognition. This prediction is supported by comparing the results of a best likeness study (Rhodes et al., 1996) and a recognition study that used the same faces (Rhodes & Tremewan, 1994). On average, 10% caricatures were the best likeness, whereas 30% and 50% caricatures were optimal for recognition. Therefore, more extreme caricatures appear to be optimal for recognition than for best likeness choices, as conjectured.

To summarise, line drawing caricatures can capture a likeness very effectively. They are generally considered as good as undistorted images and are sometimes considered the best likeness (see Table 6.2). The optimal exaggeration levels seem to be lower than for recognition, perhaps because people are reluctant to rate an obviously distorted image as a good likeness. But any such a bias does not eliminate the appeal of caricatures altogether. Overall, the results of the likeness studies are remarkably consistent with those of the recognition studies and provide strong converging evidence for the power of caricatures.

Learning

Given the effectiveness of caricatures for capturing a likeness, one might predict that they would also be effective stimuli for learning new faces. Only a few published studies have investigated this prediction and the results are mixed.

Stevenage (1995a,b) has investigated whether people learn to name caricatures more quickly than undistorted line drawings, and whether recognition of the original faces (undistorted photographs) is better when names have been learned for caricatures of those faces, than for undistorted drawings of the faces. She found that both adults (Stevenage, 1995a) and children (Stevenage, 1995b) learned names more quickly for caricatures than undistorted drawings, as would be expected given the distinctiveness of caricatures and the ease with which distinctive faces can be learned compared with more typical faces (Ellis, Shepherd, Gibling, & Shepherd, 1988). The more interesting question, however, was whether the original photographs would be recognised better after learning caricatures or undistorted drawings. Stevenage (1995a) found that the caricature-trained group recognised more of the photographs than the drawing-trained group, but only if the training was restricted, so that the caricature group learned more of the names before recognition was tested (as described above). With unlimited training, the two groups did equally well. Therefore, caricature training did not appear to facilitate recognition of the undistorted photographs. It was, however, just as effective as training with undistorted drawings, suggesting that exaggerated distinctive features can offset the effects of distortion from the original form, as in recognition studies.

There is some evidence that caricatures can facilitate recognition of undistorted faces in infants. Tyrrell, Anderson, Clubb, and Bradbury (1987) found that 30- to 35-week-old infants who studied a caricature for 40 seconds could subsequently discriminate between a photograph of that person and one of another person (of the same sex) and between that caricature and a caricature of another person. In both cases the babies looked longer at the novel face. In contrast, infants who had first studied a photograph could not subsequently discriminate a caricature of that person from one of another same-sex person. These results suggest that caricatures may be effective for learning what a face looks like, perhaps by drawing attention to its distinctive features. However, only four face pairs were used and the difference in novelty-preference between the caricature-first and photograph-first conditions was only marginally significant, so that these intriguing results need to be replicated using a more powerful design.

Other, more anecdotal, evidence that caricatures can facilitate learning comes from a mnemonist, TE, whose mnemonic strategy for remembering faces was to "try to discover at least one distinctive feature and preferably more and then try to exaggerate these" (Wilding & Valentine, 1985, p.217). This "caricaturing" strategy resulted in superior recognition performance for TE compared with controls. It should also facilitate his recognition of caricatures and it would be instructive to compare the size of any caricature advantage for these "mnemonised" faces with that obtained for faces encoded normally.

The potential of caricatures to facilitate learning of complex and unfamiliar patterns is only just beginning to be explored. Many questions remain unanswered. Can caricature-training help experts learn new members of a familiar homogeneous class, like faces or cars? Can it help novices learn to distinguish the members of an unfamiliar homogeneous class, like faces from an unfamiliar race or different passerine birds? Is it more resistant to forgetting than training with undistorted exemplars? Perhaps, being more distinctive, caricatures would be remembered better than the undistorted exemplars, and would facilitate training when information must be retained over long periods. If caricature-training can facilitate learning, then the potential for use in education would be considerasble.

Qualifications

In the studies reviewed so far, caricatures were almost always as effective as undistorted drawings. Sometimes they even functioned as superportraits. However, there are definite limits to the power of caricatures. In particular, line drawing caricatures are not recognised better than undistorted photographs (Hagen & Perkins, 1983; Tversky & Baratz, 1985). Photographs, which contain much more information about 3-D structure than line drawings (even shaded ones) and which are more familiar kinds of images than line drawing caricatures, are easier to recognise.

Two studies, which pre-dated computer caricature generators, obtained this result when artists' caricatures were pitted against photographs. The first study, by Hagen and Perkins (1983), used caricatures of previously unfamiliar faces (see Fig. 6.8), because of a concern that caricatures of public figures might be more familiar than photographs of those individuals. Subjects saw each face for three seconds, either as a caricature, a three-quarter-view photograph, or a profile photograph, and then had to pick these study faces out of a larger set of either the same type or a different type. Effective representations should be readily recognised as familiar (giving many hits), if the face has been seen before, and readily rejected as unfamiliar (giving few false alarms), if it has not been seen. Caricatures of faces seen as photographs (in the same pose) were harder to recognise (fewer hits and more false alarms) than the photographs themselves. Similar results were obtained when different views were shown in the study and test photographs. Nor did studying caricatures appear to enhance

FIG. 6.8. Examples of picture sets used by Hagen and Perkins (1983): three-quarter-view photograph (top), profile photograph (middle), and caricature (bottom). Artist: Andras Goldinger. Reproduced from Hagen and Perkins (1983) with permission.

recognition performance compared with studying photographs. When study and test faces were of the same type, hit rates were the same for caricatures and photographs, but false alarm rates were higher for caricatures than photographs, suggesting that the photographs were easier to recognise. Clearly the photographs were more effective than these artists' caricatures. However, the subjects had rather fragile memory representations of the faces (any change between study and test, even a change in viewpoint of the photograph, significantly impaired recognition) and one might ask whether a similar pattern would occur for more familiar faces.

More familiar, famous faces (see Fig. 6.9 for examples) were used in the second study, by Tversky and Baratz (1985). Once again, the artists' caricatures were generally less effective than the photographs for a variety of tasks (name recall, recognition, name–face matching, and representativeness judgements). Although subjects who saw either photographs or caricatures recalled as many names for caricatures as for photographs, subjects who saw both types of image recalled significantly more names for photographs than caricatures. Recognition (hits and correct rejections combined) was also better for photographs than caricatures, and the name–face matching responses were significantly faster for photographs than caricatures (for both matches and mismatches). Finally, the photographs were almost always rated as more representative of the person portrayed than the caricatures.

Assuming that the caricaturists who produced these stimuli were competent, the results of these studies indicate that the advantage of exaggerating distinctive information, seen when distorted and undistorted line drawing images are pitted against one another, is outweighed by the greater richness and/or familiarity of photographic quality images. But what would happen if the exaggerated images were themselves photographic images?

PHOTOGRAPHIC CARICATURES

Phil Benson and Dave Perrett of St Andrews University have asked just this question. Using their photographic caricature generator to distort photographs, they have begun to examine the effectiveness of photographic-quality caricatures. If these images pass muster, then we will have compelling evidence for the power of caricatures and an assurance that superportrait effects are not some artefact of impoverished stimuli.[3]

Pompidou

Sadat

Shah of Iran

Solzhenitsyn

FIG. 6.9. Examples of the photographs and caricatures used by Tversky and Baratz (1985). Reproduced from Tversky and Baratz (1985) with permission.

Recognition

Benson and Perrett (1991c) began by asking subjects whether or not photographic images of famous faces matched previously presented names. When the results for correct match and non-match trials were averaged together, most subjects were fastest on 16% and 32% caricatures, and the mean of the distribution, 19%, was significantly greater than 0%. There was a similar, but non-significant, trend for accuracy. However, for the matches considered on their own, there was no caricature advantage for speed or accuracy (although accuracy was near ceiling) (see Figs. 6.10 and 6.11, respectively). In fact the only significant effects were slower responses to -48% anticaricatures and 48% caricatures than to undistorted images, and more accurate responses to 32% and 48% caricatures than to corresponding anticaricatures (similar to the distinctiveness effects found for line drawing images by Rhodes et al., 1987). The caricature advantage was restricted to mismatches, with incorrect 16% caricatures rejected significantly more quickly than undistorted images, and caricatures

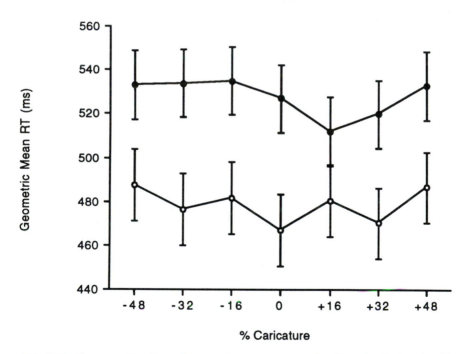

FIG. 6.10. Mean reaction times for correct responses as a function of caricature level in Benson and Perrett's (1991c) name–face matching task. Match (open circles) and non-match trials (filled circles) are plotted separately. Error bars denote 95% confidence intervals. Reproduced from Benson and Perrett (1991c) with permission.

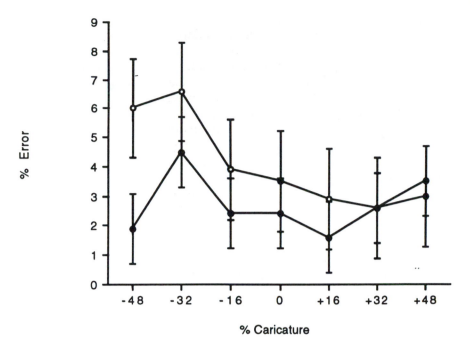

FIG. 6.11. Percentage errors as a function of caricature level in Benson and Perrett's (1991c) name–face matching task. Match (open circles) and non-match trials (filled circles) are plotted separately. Error bars denote 95% confidence intervals. Reproduced from Benson and Perrett (1991c) with permission.

(16% and 32%) rejected more quickly than corresponding anti-caricatures. The caricature advantage for detecting mismatches probably reflects the greater distinctiveness of caricatures, but caricatures need not resemble any known faces for such an effect to emerge. For example, in recognition memory experiments, new atypical faces are easier to reject than new typical faces, simply because they are less likely to resemble any of the study faces (Bartlett et al., 1984; Cohen & Carr, 1975; Going & Read, 1974; Light et al., 1979; Valentine, 1991; Valentine & Bruce, 1986a,b). Therefore, although the greater distinctiveness of caricatures allows mismatches to be detected quickly, Benson and Perrett's initial results do not show that photographic caricatures are particularly effective representations of known faces.

Research on photographic caricatures is at an early stage, and Benson and Perrett's study is the only published work on recognition of these images. Their results, suggesting that photographic caricatures may not be very effective, must be considered preliminary, however, given the small number of subjects (N = 11) and faces (N = 7) used. Other studies in the pipeline (Benson, 1995; Rhodes, Byatt, Tremewan, & Kennedy, 1996) offer a more positive view of the power of photographic caricatures.

Benson (1995) presented 50% caricatures and undistorted images of 20 famous faces to 28 subjects. The images were displayed briefly (300 msec), thereby avoiding ceiling effects, and caricatures were named significantly more quickly (M = 1.0 second) than undistorted photographs (M = 1.3 seconds). Accuracy was equal for caricatures (M = 84%) and veridicals (M = 85%). Qualitatively, these results are very similar to those of the original Stanford study with line drawing caricatures and they suggest that, like line drawing caricatures, photographic caricatures can be superportraits.

One qualification is that Benson's stimuli were preselected to include only faces that had produced a caricature advantage when shown as 50% line drawing caricatures in a previous study. Therefore, photographic caricatures may not always be superportraits, but then of course neither are line drawing caricatures. Perhaps a more serious limitation is that only the internal features of the faces were shown. Benson argues that hair is an extraneous feature, noting that prosopagnosics can sometimes use hair cues (Meadows, 1974), and that internal features are more important than external features for the recognition of familiar faces (Ellis, Shepherd, & Davies, 1979; Young et al., 1985; but see Brunas-Wagstaff, Young, & Ellis, 1992, for a failure to replicate). There is, however, considerable evidence that configural features are crucial for face recognition (see Rhodes et al., 1993 for a review), features that are disrupted when parts of the face or hair are missing. Additional studies with intact face caricatures are therefore needed to corroborate Benson's initial demonstration of the power of photographic caricatures.

We have begun to investigate the effectiveness of intact photographic caricatures in my laboratory. In our initial study, with 30 subjects and 48 famous faces, we found that people could name photographic caricatures (made using Morph) as accurately as undistorted photographs, for exaggeration levels up to 75% (the most extreme distortion tested), and as quickly as undistorted photographs, for exaggeration levels up to 45% (Rhodes, Byatt, Tremewan, & Kennedy, 1996).

Morph distorts the spatial configuration of a face to create a caricature. It does not, however, exaggerate grey-scale information (e.g. variations in brightness due to changes in pigmentation or reflectance), which also provides cues to identity (e.g. Bruce, Hanna, Dench, Healey, & Burton, 1992; Bruce, Healey, Burton, Doyle, Coombes, & Linney, 1991). Therefore, in our study, this important information was available in all the distortions for each face. This fact may explain why our anticaricatures were readily recognised, with performance only dropping below that for undistorted photographs at high levels (-60%) of distortion. We suspect that photographic caricatures in which *all* the relevant information is exaggerated may well facilitate recognition, but a test of this hypothesis will have to await further software development.

The initial studies do not offer a consensus about the power of photographic caricatures. They do show, however, that photographic caricatures can be as recognisable as undistorted photographs. They may also be superportraits for briefly presented images of internal facial features, but whether or not they can be superportraits for intact faces, remains an open question. More systematic investigation of the power of photographic caricatures is needed, especially considering the forensic potential of a superportrait effect with these images.

Likeness judgements

A handful of studies have examined how well photographic caricatures capture a likeness. Benson and Perrett (1991c) reported an overall best likeness level for famous faces of 4%, which was significantly greater than 0%, and Hadyn Ellis (1990) reported an overall best likeness level of around 6% for children judging photographic caricatures of their classmates in a pilot study. In both cases, however, the most popular choice was the veridical image, so that the results offer little support for the superportrait hypothesis, or even the equivalence of caricatures and undistorted images.

More recently, Ellis (1992) has reported a superportrait effect for photographic caricatures. He asked subjects, ranging from 4 to 21 years of age, to choose the best likeness of Kylie Minogue, star of the Australian soap, "Neighbours", which is popular with young viewers. His youngest subjects (4–6 year olds) chose a 15% caricature as the best likeness. Although intriguing, this result is difficult to interpret because no statistics were reported to show that this preferred caricature level differed significantly from 0%. Moreover, by age 10 the preference had shifted to a -10% anticaricature, and his adult subjects showed no caricature preference. A similar pattern was found for caricatures of Jason Donovan, although the age effect wasn't significant for that face.

These very preliminary results raise the possibility that subjects may be less tolerant of distortion in photographic images than in line drawings. A photograph is supposed to look just like the person, so that any noticeable distortion would count against a photographic caricature being considered a good likenesses. In contrast, line drawings make less claim to "literal" resemblance or realism, and so distortions need not count against line drawing caricatures capturing a likenesses. Recognition performance, which reflects the ability of images to access target memory representations, would be less affected by such aesthetic considerations. More research is needed before we have a clear picture of the effectiveness of photographic caricatures. Ideally, future studies should include both photographic and line drawing caricatures, given the variability found in the effectiveness of line drawing caricatures for different sets of faces (see Rhodes & Tremewan, 1994).

CONCLUDING REMARKS

In summary, caricatures seem to be as good, or better, representations than undistorted images. In some recognition studies they function as superportraits, and in others they yield equivalent performance to veridicals. Despite their obvious distortion, they are almost never less effective than veridicals, unless line drawing caricatures are pitted against richer images such as photographs. Superportrait effects have been found for various kinds of caricatures, from simple line drawings to photographic caricatures (internal features only), and for various kinds of images (familiar faces, unfamiliar faces, birds, and a variety of simple uni-dimensional stimuli used in the peak shift studies reviewed in Chapter 5). Line drawing caricatures are generally considered at least as good likenesses as undistorted images, although the preferred level of exaggeration may be less extreme than is optimal for recognition. People seem less tolerant of distortion in photographic caricatures, although such images may be still be recognised as well as normal photographs. The question of whether photographic caricatures can be superportraits for intact faces remains open.

NOTES

1. Performance was measured by the subject's ability (sensitivity) to discriminate old items from new ones, as given by the area under the memory operating characteristic (MOC) curve. An MOC curve is constructed by plotting the subject's hit rate against their false alarm rate for a range of confidence levels (i.e. degree of certainty that each test stimulus was exactly the same as one in the study set).
2. The caricatures in this study were created using two different norms for each sex—*av3*, the average of the three most typical faces of that sex, selected using typicality ratings of a large set of faces, and *avpsych*, the average of all the same-sex faces used in the study. The use of two norms was exploratory as we had no reason to think that one would be any better than the other. However, subsequent distinctiveness ratings obtained for

these norms suggest that the *avpsych* norms were better (i.e. less distinctive) than the *av3* norms. Therefore, the results shown in Fig. 6.7 are for the *avpsych* norms. Similar results were obtained for the *av3* norms, except that only the 25% caricatures and not the 50% caricatures were considered as good as the veridicals.

3. There is a tension in psychology between two research strategies. One strategy is to use simplified, briefly presented, or otherwise degraded stimuli to test the operation of a system. This strategy dominates cognitive psychology and psychophysics. Alternatively one can study a system's functioning under optimal, or at least favourable, conditions, as advocated by J.J. Gibson and other proponents of the "ecological approach". The study of caricature recognition is clearly in the spirit of the first approach. By using deliberately distorted images we hope to find out something about the nature of the underlying mental representations and recognition processes. Not only are the images deliberately distorted, but they are often highly simplified, lacking much of the information normally available in faces (e.g. depth information is minimal and motion, colour, and texture cues are virtually absent), although it would prejudge the issue to suppose that they lack *relevant* information for recognition. Indeed, we know that line drawings make explicit edge information that is critical for visual recognition (e.g. Marr, 1982) and Hildreth and Ullman (1989, p.584) note that, "a line sketch of an image often conveys most of the essential information". Biederman's (1987) theory of human image understanding, recognition-by-components, is also based on the idea that recognition depends largely on information derived from edges, and support for this view comes from studies showing that line drawings and coloured photographs are named (at the basic level) equally quickly, even when colour is diagnostic of an object's identity (e.g. yellow bananas) (Biederman & Ju, 1988). Although basic level identification (dog versus chair versus car) appears to be based on edge-representations, we don't know whether this is also true for identification of highly homogeneous stimuli such as faces. In fact the poor recognisability of line drawing caricatures and other line drawing images of faces (Davies et al., 1978) suggests that it may not be; see Roth and Bruce (1995) for a review of other evidence that surface properties may be important for face recognition. Therefore, it is important to investigate caricature effects with richer photographic images.

CHAPTER SEVEN

Caricatures and face recognition

... it is not really the perception of likeness for which we are originally programmed, but the noticing of unlikeness, the departure from the norm which stands out and sticks in the mind.

Gombrich (1972) p.13

We have seen that caricatures can facilitate the recognition of complex multidimensional stimuli like faces, as well as much simpler stimuli. Indeed the power of exaggerated or supernormal stimuli can be seen in many natural communication systems, as well as in the laboratory. I turn now to the question of how such distorted images can be so effective. The peak shift studies described in Chapter 5 offer an important clue as to how to approach this question. They showed that questions about the power of caricatures are intimately bound up with questions about mental representation. In this chapter I treat the two issues jointly, asking what our mental representations of faces are like and why caricatures are so effective.

Are caricatures easy to recognise simply because of their distinctiveness, or do they match our memory representations of faces in some more specific way? Perhaps those representations code how each face differs from a norm or average face, which is precisely the information exaggerated in a caricature. Perhaps our memory representations are themselves caricatured. I will also examine whether or not caricatures exploit some special feature of the face recognition system, and whether or not their effectiveness requires expertise.

A TOUR OF FACE SPACE

Faces are a highly homogeneous class of stimuli, all having more or less the same component parts in the same basic arrangement. Yet each face is a unique variation on the face theme, and we can recognise many thousands of them, sometimes even distinguishing the faces of so-called "identical" twins. Many studies have tried to determine how we manage this feat by examining the facial features that are used for recognition. Early cue salience studies focused on nameable features and identified the eyes, mouth, chin, and to a lesser extent the nose as important (e.g. Haig, 1985; for reviews see Rhodes, 1988; Shepherd, Davies & Ellis, 1981). More recent studies have highlighted the importance of spatial relationships between these components (e.g. Bartlett & Searcy, 1993; Carey, 1992; Carey & Diamond, 1977; Diamond & Carey, 1986; Farah et al., 1994; Haig, 1984; Rhodes, 1988; Rhodes et al., 1993; Searcy & Bartlett, 1996; Sergent, 1984a,b).

As a result of these studies we know a lot about the kind of information that is used to recognise faces. We know much less, however, about how the visual system identifies and mentally represents these distinctive features. In the next section I will consider a possible solution to this homogeneity problem, suggested by the power of caricatures. Let me begin, however, by describing a general framework within which face perception and recognition can be explored (for a more detailed account see Valentine, 1991).

Memory representations of faces can be thought of as located in a psychological face space, whose dimensions correspond to those features that we use to distinguish and recognise faces. Examples might include measures that characterise the appearance and spatial arrangement of the internal features (eyes, nose and mouth) and the face outline and hair. More categorical or isolated feature measures, such as the colour and texture of hair or the presence/absence of facial hair and glasses, are difficult to incorporate into this kind of framework and might have to be coded separately.

The spatial arrangement of representations in face space reflects the similarity of the faces, and a perceived face is recognised if it matches one of these stored representations. (This is discussed in greater detail in the Recognition and classification section.) The average face would lie at the centre of the distribution of face representations. Of course the average face might not exist in reality, or even in our imaginations, but if it did then it would occupy a central position within the space. The distribution of faces around this central point is not uniform. Typical faces are more numerous than distinctive or unusual faces, so that the density of faces should decrease with distance from the average face.

I have talked about a single face space, but we might have several such spaces, one for each structurally different class of faces of which we have experience. For example, if different features are important for distinguishing male and female faces, or faces from different racial groups, then different spaces might be used for these groups. The development of multiple spaces would presumably be a product of expertise. For example, faces from an unfamiliar race could initially be represented in an existing, own-race face space, with inappropriate features used to code the faces, so that the other-race faces form a cluster and are difficult to distinguish. With increasing experience, a more appropriate set of dimensions may be discovered and used to define a new face space.

Representing faces in face space

To recognise faces, we must code features that capture subtle variations in the shared facial configuration. As noted above, many of these features describe complex spatial relations between parts of the face. But how are they coded? Two different kinds of account are possible within the face space framework. In developing these accounts, I will draw heavily on the work of Tim Valentine and his colleagues (Valentine, 1991; Valentine & Endo, 1992), although the ideas presented here differ somewhat from theirs.

One view is that we code the absolute values of each face on some fixed set of features that are useful for distinguishing faces. For example, we might use features that vary widely in a population. Faces are then represented as *points* in a face space whose dimensions correspond to the features used to encode faces. I will refer to this view as the *absolute coding* model, although Valentine (1991) has used the term *exemplar model*, to contrast this account with an alternative *norm-based coding* account.

Another view is that variations in the facial configuration that distinguish different individuals may be represented in a norm-based coding scheme (Goldstein & Chance, 1980; Hebb, 1949; Hochberg, 1978; Rhodes et al., 1987; Rhodes & McLean, 1990; Valentine & Bruce, 1986b; Valentine, 1991). The idea that norms play a role in encoding faces can be instantiated in a variety of ways. For example, a norm could be used to weight features according to distinctiveness, or to code explicitly how each feature value deviates from the average value (e.g. X units above the mean value, or X standard deviation units above the mean value).

Or the norm could be used to select only the most distinctive features for coding, capturing the intuition that something may only really become a feature when it deviates from the norm (Brennan, 1982; Gombrich, 1960). Faces could be represented as points in a space with the norm at the origin, or perhaps as vectors originating from the norm, as suggested by Valentine (1991).

Norm-based coding offers a clever solution to the homogeneity problem, because the shared configuration that makes faces difficult for a part-based recognition system is exploited to generate a norm that provides an ideal comparison point against which to assess the unique distinguishing features of each individual face. Norm-based coding is also a very plausible hypothesis given that we seem able to abstract norms for faces (Bruce et al., 1991; Inn, Walden, & Solso, 1993; Reed, 1972; Solso & McCarthy, 1981a,b; Strauss, 1979 – a more detailed review appears later in this chapter). Indeed this ability may even be part of our innate endowment. In addition to having knowledge of the structure of faces, i.e. the arrangement of eyes, nose and mouth within the head (Goren, Sarty, & Wu, 1975; Johnson, Dziurawiec, Ellis & Morton, 1991; Johnson & Morton, 1991; Morton & Johnson, 1991), neonates also seem able to form prototypes of the faces they see (Walton & Bower, 1993).[1] Therefore, we may come equipped with an innate face template that can be continuously updated to represent a running average of experienced faces, i.e. a norm.

Recognition and classification

How does recognition occur in face space? The basic idea is that a face will be recognised if its perceptual representation matches one of the stored representations in face space. The more closely the perceptual input resembles the target representation, and the less it resembles neighbouring distractors, the better recognition performance will be. Valentine (1991) also notes that there is likely to be some error associated with coding the input, which will increase as viewing conditions deteriorate, and that recognition performance will deteriorate as the error increases.

What is not so clear is how similarity should be represented in face space. The most straightforward view is that (dis)similarity depends simply on the Euclidean distance separating point representations in face space, as suggested by Valentine (1991) for absolute coding.[2] However, for norm-based coding, the angular distance between representations might also play a role, in addition to Euclidean distance. For example, similarity might be some weighted function of angle and Euclidean distance, such as, $w_1 cosine(angle)/w_2 distance$. A purely vector-based similarity measure is unsatisfactory because it implies that the caricatures of two faces are as similar to each other as the two undistorted representations (or even the two anticaricatures) of those faces, which is clearly not the case. However, by allowing angular distance to contribute as well as Euclidean distance, we can capture the notion that the way a face deviates from the norm, i.e. its direction from the norm, might provide crucial information for recognition.[3]

In addition to assuming different measures of similarity, the models also differ in their accounts of how faces are classified as a face (rather than a jumbled face). In absolute coding, Valentine (1991) suggests that decisions are made by comparing each pattern with neighbouring faces, so that classification speed increases with the density of neighbouring exemplars in some (unspecified) local region. In norm-based coding, he suggests that decisions are made by comparing the patterns with a norm, so that the closer a face is to the norm, the more quickly it will be classified as a face (see later for a critical discussion of the role of norms or prototypes in categorisation generally).

The effects of distinctiveness on face recognition and classification can be understood as density effects in both models. Faces rated as more distinctive are recognised better than more typical faces (see Johnston & Ellis, 1995 for a recent review), because the former have fewer close neighbours than the latter. In contrast, distinctive faces are harder to classify as a face than are typical faces (Valentine, 1991), because they have fewer neighbours. Similarity is measured differently in the two models, but in both cases, typical faces lie in more crowded regions of face space than more distinctive faces.

Density effects can also explain the finding that inversion disrupts recognition of typical faces more than distinctive faces (Valentine, 1991), if it is assumed that inversion increases the error of coding. An increase in this error will disrupt recognition more for faces with closer neighbours, i.e. more for typical than distinctive faces. In contrast, when faces don't need to be distinguished, as in a face classification task, no interaction between inversion and distinctiveness is predicted, and none is found (Valentine, 1991).

Another factor that influences face recognition is the race of a face. Many studies have found that faces from an unfamiliar race are harder to recognise than own-race faces (for a review, see Bothwell, Brigham, & Malpass, 1989). The absolute coding model accounts for this effect by supposing that other-race faces are more densely clustered than own-race faces in face space. But given that people know very few faces from an unfamiliar race, it seems unlikely that those faces would be more densely clustered than own-race faces. Moreover, if other-race faces are more densely clustered, then they should be easier to classify as faces than own-race faces, because classification depends on local density on the absolute coding view. There is, however, no empirical support for this prediction. Valentine (1991) found that white subjects took longer to classify black faces than white faces, and Valentine and Endo (1992) found no difference in the speed with which British (white) and Japanese subjects classified own- and other-race faces.[4] The absolute coding model therefore has some difficulty accounting for race effects in face processing. In contrast norm-based coding can readily account for these effects. Faces from an unfamiliar race are difficult to recognise because they all differ from the (own-race) norm in the same way, and are slower to classify as faces because they are further from the norm than own-race faces (see Hebb, 1949, p.116 for a similar suggestion).

Both models can account for a variety of effects in face processing, although race effects may be handled better by a norm-based coding account. In addition to the empirical evidence, more general considerations may also be relevant in weighing up these two models. On the one hand, norm-based coding models may be less parsimonious than absolute coding models (although we will see in the next section that the economy of exemplar-only models comes at a price), leading some to prefer absolute coding. On the other hand, comparisons with a norm provide an ideal way of coding the subtle variations in a shared configuration that distinguish individual faces, whereas absolute coding offers no account of how we solve this homogeneity problem. On balance, then, comparison with a norm remains an attractive hypothesis about how faces and other homogeneous objects are mentally represented.

The idea that norms might play an important role in mental representation is not new. Norms, and the closely related concepts of schemata and prototypes, have a distinguished history in the development of ideas about mental representation (Attneave, 1954; Bartlett, 1932; Head, 1920; Hebb, 1949; Woodworth, 1938—see also Oldfield & Zangwill, 1942, 1943 for an early survey of usage of the schema concept in psychology). In the next section I will review some of this material, before turning to the question of what role norms might play in recognising caricatures.

AN HISTORICAL (DE)TOUR— NORMS AND RELATED NOTIONS

Norms, and the related notions of schemata and prototypes, have played a major role in understanding a variety of phenomena, from control of movements to categorisation. The key idea, which comes up again and again, is that some kind of average or central tendency provides an ideal reference point against which to compare incoming stimuli.

Movement

The physiologist Head (1920) first coined the term "schema", using it to refer to the ongoing average context within which experience is embedded. His special interest was in movement and postural control, and he argued that rather than being coded in some fixed frame of reference, movements must be computed with reference to a representation of current postural state or *schema*. He asserted that, "Every new posture or movement is recorded on this plastic schema" (Head, 1920, pp. 606), which is then updated to reflect the new state.

Memory

Ten years later, inspired by Head's theory, Bartlett (1932) gave schemata a crucial role in memory, arguing that schema theory, "points the way to a satisfactory solution of the phenomenon of remembering in the full sense" (Bartlett, 1932, p.199). Rejecting the idea of static memory traces, he proposed instead that remembering is based on malleable schemata (see Oldfield, 1954 for a review). By a memory schema he meant, "an active organisation of past reactions, or of past experiences ... All incoming impulses of a certain kind, or mode, go together to build up an active, organised setting: visual, auditory, various types of cutaneous impulses and the like, at a relatively low level; all the experiences connected by a common interest; in literature, history, art, science, philosophy and so on, at a higher level" (Bartlett, 1932, p. 201). Remembering, according to Bartlett, consists largely of inferring what events must have occurred to produce the current schema, as if the organism worked out that, "this and this must have occurred, in order that my present state should be what it is" (op. cit., p.202). Bartlett's legacy can be seen in modern theories of memory that emphasise constructive processes (see Alba & Hasher, 1983 for a critical review).

Shape

By 1938, schemata had taken on an additional role in the mental representation of visual form. Woodworth proposed that unfamiliar shapes are represented as a "schema, with correction". However, his schema could be any familiar stimulus, rather than an amalgam or average of previously experienced stimuli, as in the Head/Bartlett conception. For example, to remember an unfamiliar nonsense figure, you might note both its similarity to some familiar form or object and how it deviates from that form. Woodworth saw this schema plus correction process as a fundamental method of assimilating new experience, and marshalled evidence for it in his 1938 text on experimental psychology. He cited research showing that regular figures (requiring no correction – e.g. semicircle, circle, square) and figures requiring only simple corrections (e.g. a triangle with a gap at each corner, an oblong with a gap in one of the long sides) are among the easiest to learn, and that reproductions from memory show evidence of assimilation to a norm or schema and exaggeration of distinctive features (but see Hebb & Foord, 1945, for a critique of studies using repeated reproduction).

The notion of a schema as the central tendency of a class of exemplars reappears later in theories of perception, (Hebb, 1949; Helson, 1947, 1964) and when combined with Woodworth's schema-plus-correction method for representing form (Attneave, 1954, 1957) the result is a norm-based coding hypothesis. Fred Attneave did just this and proposed that similar items could be economically coded by noting how they differ "from some skeleton pattern which includes the communalities of the group" (1954, p.190). He cited the example of faces from an unfamiliar racial group, conjecturing that they are difficult to recognise because we try to code them using a norm that is not central for those stimuli. Coded against a Caucasian norm, all Chinese faces will deviate in a similar direction and so will tend to look the same.

Many have recognised that norm-based coding offers an elegant and economical solution to the homogeneity problem (Attneave, 1954, 1957; Hochberg, 1978; Oldfield, 1954). However, Attneave (1957) also recognised that it is not the only way that similar stimuli could be coded. Alternatively, as we saw in Chapter 5, they could simply be coded on some set of absolute dimensions (not relative to a norm) or one could note how each deviates from each of the other exemplars, rather than from the central tendency of the class. Attneave therefore sought support for the norm-based coding hypothesis, by testing a prediction (which he attributes to Hebb, 1949) that follows from it, namely that learning a set of unfamiliar patterns should be facilitated if subjects know the central tendency of the class. Consistent with his prediction, pretraining on the prototype reduced the number of errors made in the course of learning to identify the exemplars. Clear facilitation was obtained for learning letter matrices (Experiment 1) and 6- or 12-sided polygons (Experiment 2). Pretraining was especially helpful when the polygons varied on a fixed rather than a random subset of points, consistent with the idea that a norm is used to find the distinctive features. Of course, if norm-based coding is a basic tool for representing stimuli that vary around a prototype, then the control subjects may well have extracted the prototype too. As Attneave says, we can only assume that subjects who received pretraining on the prototype had a head start in learning the patterns. He also suggested repeating these studies using a non-central standard to see if the centrality of the norm was important. Twenty years later Eleanor Rosch (1973a) did precisely that and found that centrality was indeed important (see Categorisation section for details).

Abstracting the central tendency

In Attneave's study, subjects were shown a prototype for the exemplars to be learned. However, prototypes are not normally given, so if they are to be used to distinguish similar patterns they must be abstracted from experienced exemplars. In the next decade numerous studies investigated whether prototypes are indeed abstracted from experience with exemplars (see Reed, 1973, for a review). In many of these studies subjects were trained to *group* exemplars together into a common category, rather than to individuate exemplars within a category, but similar prototype abstraction effects seem to occur whether the focus is on categorisation or individual recognition.

Posner and Keele (1968, 1970) were among the first to study prototype abstraction during category learning. After learning to classify dot patterns that were distortions of a prototype (either a triangle or letter shape or a random pattern), their subjects classified the prototypes as quickly and accurately as the learned exemplars, and more quickly and accurately than new exemplars that were equally distant from the learned exemplars (Posner & Keele, 1968). Although these results suggest that the subjects had abstracted prototypes, they may not have done so during learning. Instead they may simply have recognised the prototype as a good exemplar when they saw it at test. Posner and Keele's (1970) subjects, however, forgot most of the studied exemplars over the course of a week, yet the prototype effects remained —suggesting that the prototype was abstracted during learning. Posner and Keele (1968, 1970) used dot patterns, but similar prototype effects have also been obtained with more meaningful stimuli, including schematic faces (Reed, 1972).

Connectionist networks also appear to abstract prototypes. For example, the "mate recognition" networks described in Chapter 5 preferred a symmetric pattern that was the average of a set of asymmetric training patterns (Johnstone, 1994). Moreover, the preference for this novel, symmetric pattern was just as strong as when that pattern was included in the training set. This result suggests that an abstract averaging process can be as powerful as experience in shaping the network's response to an average pattern.

A prototype also appears to be abstracted when subjects individuate the exemplars in a category, rather than grouping them under a common category label. Franks and Bransford (1971) had their subjects reproduce arrays of geometric forms, created by applying various transformations to a base pattern. In a surprise recognition test the prototype, which had never been seen, received the highest confidence rating as a previously seen pattern and ratings for other new exemplars increased with their similarity to the prototype. Other studies have found similar pseudo-memory for prototypes for geometric figures (Solso & Raynis, 1979), Identikit faces (Inn et al., 1993; Solso & McCarthy, 1981a), computer-generated (Mac-a-Mug Pro) faces (Bruce, Doyle, Dench, & Burton, 1991) and three-digit numbers (Solso & McCarthy, 1981b). Furthermore, the prototype was considered equally familiar as the old exemplars for the geometric figures and numbers, and more familiar than the old exemplars for the faces (Bransford and Franks only compared the prototype with new exemplars).

Categorisation

These and many other studies led to the idea that prototypes might be used to represent categories (for a recent review see Hampton, 1993). For example, Franks and Bransford (1971) interpreted their results as evidence that a category is represented by a schema specifying a prototype plus allowable deviations (specified by transformation rules). The idea that prototypes are used to represent categories provides an appealing account of some curious aspects of natural, everyday categories. For example, not all exemplars are considered equally good members of the category[5], not all attributes are considered equally important for defining membership, many categories lack clear boundaries (for a review see Eysenck & Keane, 1990) and many seem to lack necessary defining attributes (for a review see Hampton, 1993). These characteristics squarely contradict the classical notion that categories are mentally represented as sets of necessary and sufficient defining attributes (e.g. Frege, 1952), whereas they follow naturally from the idea that concepts are organised around central prototypes, with category membership determined by similarity to the prototype (e.g. Rosch 1973a,b,c, 1975, 1978; see also Barsalou, 1985; Hampton, 1993).

Further evidence that concepts might be organised around prototypes came from studies on colour categories inspired by work in anthropology. Anthropologists had found that although languages vary in their number of colour terms, their basic terms[6] all come from a set of eleven, which in English are black, white, red, green, yellow, blue, brown, purple, pink, orange and grey (Berlin & Kay, 1969). They also found that there was considerable cross-cultural agreement about the *focal* colours for each colour category, whether or not people had colour terms for the categories. These results were followed up by the psychologist Eleanor Rosch (1975), working with Dani people in New Guinea. She found that focal colours were remembered better than non-focal colours (again, whether or not people had names for them), that names were learned more quickly for focal than non-focal colours and that colour categories were learned more quickly when the focal colour was central than when it was peripheral to the range of exemplars (Rosch, 1973a). Similar results were obtained with American children (Rosch, 1973b). Prototypical shapes (square, circle and equilateral triangle) were also learned more quickly than non-prototypical ones and shape categories were learned more quickly when the hypothesised prototype was central to the range of distortions seen than when it was peripheral (Rosch, 1973a). These results all point to the idea that perceptual categories like colour and shape are organised around focal or prototypical instances.

Additional support for the prototype view comes from studies spanning a wide range of natural and artificial categories that are not as physiologically determined as colour categories (see Eysenck & Keane, 1990 for a review). For example, people consistently rate the typicality of category members differentially and these ratings predict their reaction times to classify the exemplars (for a review see Smith and Medin, 1981). Typical exemplars tend to be learned first (Rosch 1973b), to be mentioned first when listing category exemplars (Battig & Montague, 1969; Mervis, Catlin, & Rosch, 1976) and to be drawn when asked to sketch an exemplar (Rosch, Simpson, & Miller, 1976). All these findings are consistent with the idea that some form of prototype plays a central role in the organisation of many categories.[7]

There has been considerable debate about the nature of prototypes. They could be "focal" or typical category members (e.g. Rosch, 1973a) or some more abstract representation, such as the central tendency or average of a set of exemplars (e.g. Attneave, 1957; Posner & Keele, 1968; Reed, 1972) or the modal (most frequent) combination of attributes (e.g. Neumann, 1974; Solso & McCarthy, 1981a,b).[8] Indeed there may be considerable flexibility in the nature of prototypes, with different sorts used for different categories (for discussions see MacLaury, 1991; Medin & Smith, 1984; Smith & Medin, 1981). For example, a spatial average such as the average outline shape might well be computed for basic level categories (e.g. bird, dog, house, chair), whose members have a similar part structure (Tversky & Hemenway, 1984) and overall shape (Rosch, Mervis, Gray, Johnson, & Boyes-Bream, 1976), but would be impossible to construct for superordinate categories (e.g. furniture, fruit), whose members are heterogeneous in shape and whose commonality rests more on functional than perceptual attributes. An averaged prototype would be especially suitable for homogeneous categories like faces whose exemplars share a configuration, having the same basic parts in the same basic arrangement.

Whatever form a prototype takes, its centrality to the category is important. Attneave (1957) predicted that this might be the case, and this was confirmed by Rosch's (1973a) finding that perceptual categories are learned more quickly when the prototype is central to the set of exemplars than when it is peripheral. A central prototype makes good sense for a theory of category representation, providing a built-in mechanism for the graded nature of categories with typicality diminishing as members differ more from the prototype. It is also consistent with the idea that norms or prototypes play a direct role in the representation and recognition of exemplars. If, as claimed by the norm-based coding hypothesis, we sometimes represent exemplars in terms of how they deviate from a norm or prototype, then a centrally located norm would be better than a peripheral one, because a peripheral norm reduces the range of possible deviation-directions. Recall the situation in which an own-race norm is used to encode other-race faces. Because that norm is peripheral to the other-race faces they all deviate from it in a similar direction and tend to look the same.

The last decade has seen a vigorous, and as yet unresolved, debate about whether prototypes are really abstracted and used to categorise exemplars. Many have challenged the idea that prototypes play any role in categorisation at all (for reviews see Medin & Smith, 1984; Smith & Medin, 1981), suggesting instead that category membership is determined by an exemplar's overall (average) similarity to the members of one category relative to others (e.g. Medin & Schaffer, 1978; Nosofsky, 1988). An exemplar is considered to belong to the category whose members it most closely resembles. On this exemplar-only view, prototypes are falsely recognised because their centrality ensures a relatively high overall level of similarity to the stored exemplars.

There is a clear trade-off between representational and processing economy in the two kinds of models. Exemplar models have representational economy because there is no need for an explicitly represented prototype. However, this economy comes at the expense of reduced processing efficiency, because category membership is now determined on the basis of multiple comparisons (possibly in parallel) with exemplars. In contrast, prototype models offer much greater processing efficiency, with category membership decided by comparison with a single prototype or ideal, at the cost of a small reduction in representational economy. Rather than computing the similarity of an exemplar to all the stored exemplars, only its similarity to the prototype needs to be computed. Such considerations will not, however, determine who is right about all this. What, then, is the evidence?

In a recent review of the evidence Medin and Florian (1992) concluded that exemplar models consistently fare better than prototype models.

For example, Medin and Schaffer (1978) showed that category learning and transfer were determined by proximity to exemplars, not by distance from central tendencies, and Hintzman (1986; Hintzman & Ludlum, 1980) has shown that so-called prototype effects, such as faster forgetting of exemplars than prototypes, can be produced in models that only store exemplars. Perhaps prototypes are not abstracted during category learning at all, or if they are they do not guide categorisation decisions. Estes (1986) favours the latter view: "What I think we can conclude with some confidence is that although prototypes may, under some circumstances, be formed during category learning, they need not, and probably generally do not, enter into categorisation judgments in the way assumed in extant prototype models" (op. cit., p.171).

These negative views about prototypes have been challenged recently by the success of several connectionist models of categorisation (e.g. Gluck & Bower, 1988; McClelland & Rumelhart, 1985; Shanks, 1991a—see also the connectionist recognition models described in Chapter 5). In contrast to exemplar models, these networks keep no record of specific training exemplars. The entire set of weights is a composite of all the training patterns, and so in this sense the networks are prototype models. Take Shanks' (1991a) model as an example. The network consists of an input layer of units, each representing a (binary) feature of the exemplar to be categorised, connected in parallel to a layer of output units representing the categories. Feature-category associations are therefore used to activate categories, and during learning, the weights between units are adjusted to increase the probability of making correct categorisations.

Shanks thinks that prototype models have been prematurely dismissed, arguing that much of the so-called evidence against prototype models is actually quite consistent with such models. Turning the arguments against prototype effects on their heads, he argues that so-called exemplar effects can actually be generated by prototype models! For instance, the fact that similarity of test items to training exemplars facilitates classification performance has been taken as evidence against prototype models (e.g. Homa, Sterling, & Trepel, 1981). However, Shanks argues that the connectionist prototype model can also produce this similarity effect because the specific training stimuli have an effect on the final weight matrix that generalises to new, similar test exemplars (Shanks, 1991b).

An innovative set of priming studies by Barbara Malt (1989) also warns against dismissing prototypes. She reasoned that if similar exemplars are activated during categorisation of a target then subsequent categorisation of those exemplars should be facilitated or primed. In contrast, if categorisation depends on comparison with a prototype then no priming would be expected (beyond that due to spreading activation or perceptual facilitation). Her priming results suggested that *both* strategies were used (see below).

In summary the debate about whether or not prototypes are used to represent categories and decide category membership continues. Indeed there may not be a clear winner, with many of the participants acknowledging that categorisation may be flexible enough to exploit both exemplars and prototypes (e.g. Elio & Anderson, 1981; Hampton, 1993; Homa et al., 1981; Malt, 1989; Medin 1986; Medin, Altom, & Murphy, 1984). For example, exemplar comparisons might dominate the early stages of category learning with prototype comparisons taking over as more exemplars are experienced (for discussion see Homa et al., 1981[9]; Homa, Goldhardt, Burruel-Homa, & Carson Smith, 1993). Typicality might also affect the preferred strategy, with prototype comparisons favoured for typical exemplars and exemplar comparisons for atypical exemplars (Malt, 1989). There is certainly no difficulty finding a mechanism by which both exemplars and prototypes could be coded. For example, relatively similar exemplars could be averaged, but more dissimilar exemplars kept distinct (Bruce et al., 1991). Alternatively, one could store distinct representations of all the exemplars, as well as keeping a running average. Such a dual representation system might offend standards of parsimony, but it could be an ideal way to cope with the conflicting demands of categorisation (find commonalities) and individual recognition (find distinctive information).

Even if prototypes are not used much in categorisation, they do seem to be abstracted, which raises the question of what they are abstracted *for*, if not to make categorisation judgements (Estes, 1986)? One possibility is that norms or prototypes feature in the visual system's solution to the homogeneity problem. Perhaps, as suggested earlier, they are used to individuate the members of homogeneous categories, by providing critical reference points against which the distinctive features of individuals can be coded.

UNDERSTANDING CARICATURE EFFECTS IN FACE SPACE

We saw earlier that there are two views of how faces are mentally represented in face space. The absolute coding view argues that faces are represented as absolute values on a set of relevant features, the norm-based coding view that norms play some role in the representation of faces. In this section I will consider how these two views account for the power of caricatures, and whether they can be empirically distinguished. First, however, I want to consider a simpler hypothesis about the power of caricatures: one that is compatible with either view.

The caricatured trace hypothesis

Caricatures would be easy to recognise, and anticaricatures difficult to recognise, if our memory representations of faces were themselves caricatured. Caricatures would also be considered good likenesses of faces. On this view caricatures are effective because they match the stored representations more closely than do undistorted images. This caricatured trace proposal, which draws on classic processes of schematisation and exaggeration in long-term memory (e.g. Bartlett, 1932; Koffka, 1935), has appealed to a number of theorists (J. J. Gibson, 1947; Rhodes et al., 1987; Tversky & Baratz, 1985).

How can we test this hypothesis? One source of evidence might come from people's attempts to draw faces from memory. Do these drawings contain distortions indicative of exaggerated memory traces? Except for J.J. Gibson's exploratory study with aircraft drawings no-one has attempted a production study. The complexity of faces and the minimal drawing skills possessed by most of us mean that the subjects in such a study would probably have to be artists.

An alternative might be to devise a computer-assisted "production" study, where people could generate images without any drawing skills. This is exactly what Benson and Perrett (1994) did in their likeness study, discussed in the previous chapter. Their subjects controlled the level of distortion of computer-generated line drawings of famous faces and consistently selected caricatures as the optimal likeness. This result is consistent with the idea that familiar faces are caricatured in memory. If other studies in which subjects select the best likeness from a set of images (reviewed in Chapter 6) are also interpreted as assisted-production studies, then their results can be interpreted in the same way. Unfortunately, an alternative interpretation of such studies is possible, namely that people simply produce or select the image that is most recognisable. Rather than being an externalisation of the mental representation, the image selected might simply be the one that is most effective for accessing that representation.

How else might we try to test the caricatured trace account? My colleagues and I have suggested that if memory traces become caricatured by processes of schematisation and exaggeration operating in long-term memory, then a superportrait effect should be restricted to relatively familiar faces (Rhodes et al., 1987). Initial findings favoured the caricatured trace account, with no hint of a superportrait effect for unfamiliar faces. Undistorted images of unfamiliar faces were considered better likenesses than caricatures (Rhodes et al., 1987), and were recognised more quickly than caricatures (Rhodes & Moody, 1990). Moreover, even for familiar faces, the effectiveness of caricatures seemed to increase with familiarity of the faces, with more extreme caricatures considered optimal for more familiar than for less familiar famous faces (Benson & Perrett, 1991c).

More recently, however, superportrait effects have been found for unfamiliar faces (Mauro & Kubovy, 1992; Rhodes & Tremewan, 1994). For example, Rhodes and Tremewan found that enhanced line drawing caricatures of a group of classmates' faces were identified more accurately than undistorted images, whether or not the subjects knew the faces prior to the experiment. Familiarity beyond that needed to label a face was not required for caricatures to be effective. Therefore, the power of caricatures cannot depend on processes operating in long-term memory, as proposed by the caricatured trace account.

These results do not rule out the possibility that distorted mental representations contribute to the power of caricatures. Mauro and Kubovy (1992) found that people take longer to say "different" to a caricature following an unfamiliar face than to a face following a caricature of that face, and interpreted this result as evidence that we select and amplify a face's distinctive features from the outset. If this interpretation is correct, and our *perceptual* representations of faces are caricatured, then the power of caricatures might indeed be due to caricatured mental representations. Alternatively, Mauro and Kubovy's result might mean that more distinctive versions of faces (e.g. caricatures) can access the undistorted representations of those faces more effectively than can less distinctive versions (e.g. anticaricatures). In the next section we will consider how such a distinctiveness effect might contribute to the power of caricatures.

Caricature effects in an absolute coding model

We saw from the peak shift studies described in Chapter 5 that when stimuli are simply coded as absolute values on some dimension(s), caricatures derive their power from their distinctiveness. On this view, caricatures are easy to recognise because they lie in less densely populated regions of face space than undistorted images. A caricature may not match the target representation as well as the undistorted face, because it lies further from it, but its increased distance from the target is offset by the lower density of distractors around the more distinctive caricature. If the advantage from this reduction in density of distractors outweighs the disadvantage of being further from the target, then a caricature will be a superportrait. If the two trade off about equally then a caricature will be just as recognisable as an undistorted image.

Anticaricatures will be difficult to recognise because they are not only further from their targets than the corresponding undistorted images, but are also located in more crowded regions of face space.

Caricature effects in a norm-based coding model

On a norm-based coding view, the most straightforward interpretation of the power of caricatures is to suppose that they exaggerate the very features that we use to recognise faces. Superportraits can be created by explicitly exaggerating how each face differs from a norm. Therefore, the important features for recognition capture how a face deviates from a norm. As we saw earlier, this norm-deviation information could be encoded in a variety of ways, and the precise mechanism by which caricatures facilitate recognition will depend on exactly which model is adopted. But the general idea is that caricatures are effective because they make salient how each face differs from a norm, not simply because they lie in less densely populated regions of face space.

Are face caricature effects solely distinctiveness effects?

Recently, my colleagues and I have tried to determine whether or not the power of caricatures comes entirely from their distinctiveness, i.e. from their location in relatively sparsely populated regions of face space. If it does, then the recognisability of an image should depend only on its (Euclidean) distance from the target and neighbouring distractors. There should be no effect of how closely its direction from the norm matches that of the target. In contrast, if a face is coded relative to a norm, then such directional information may be important, in addition to distance. Norm-deviation vectors, radiating out from the origin, might define psychologically privileged directions in face space, so that two images lying on the same vector will appear more similar than two images separated by an equal distance, but lying on different vectors.

We tested the "distinctiveness-only" hypothesis by comparing recognition of caricatures, undistorted images, anticaricatures, and a new kind of distortion, "lateral" caricatures, which shift faces "sideways" in face space (Fig. 7.1). Caricatures, anticaricatures and laterals are all equally distorted (in terms of Euclidean distance) from the original faces, but because the density of faces decreases with distance from the origin, the laterals lie in a region of lower density than anticaricatures, but higher density than caricatures. Therefore, on the absolute coding view, laterals should be recognised better than anticaricatures, but worse than caricatures. To the extent that norm-deviation direction information is important, however, recognition of the laterals will suffer.

We asked our subjects (N = 24) to identify a caricature, an anticaricature, four laterals[10], (all 50% distortions) and an undistorted

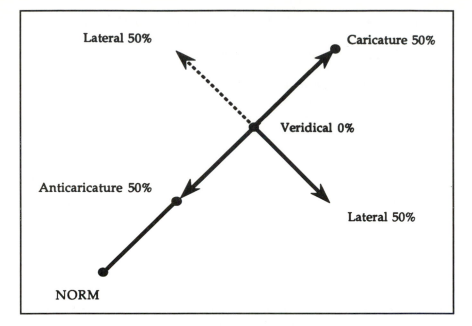

FIG. 7.1. Shows how a point on an undistorted face (Veridical 0%) moves in a caricature, anticaricature, and lateral caricature. The corresponding point on the norm (NORM) is found (e.g. the tip of the nose on the two faces would be corresponding points) and the point on the face is moved relative to that norm point. In a 50% caricature the point on the face is moved 50% further away from the corresponding point on the norm, in the direction of the vector joining the two points. In a 50% anticaricature the point is moved 50% back along that vector towards the corresponding point on the norm. In the lateral caricature the point is moved orthogonally to the vector in one of the two possible directions shown. The choice of direction for the lateral move was constrained to reflect the bilateral symmetry of the face. All the points on the left side of the face moved the same way (either left or right, with respect to the norm-deviation direction) as did all points on the right side of the face. This resulted in four laterals for each face.

image for each of 28 famous faces (Rhodes, Carey, Byatt, & Proffitt, 1996). A complete set of distortions for one face is shown in Fig. 7.2. As usual, caricatures were recognised as accurately (M = 56%) as undistorted images (M = 54%), and both were recognised significantly better than anticaricatures (M = 33%). Most interestingly, recognition of the laterals was significantly better (M = 47%) than anticaricatures, but worse than caricatures or undistorted faces.[11] Similar results were obtained in a second study, in which subjects learned to identify unfamiliar faces before being tested on recognition of the different kinds of distortion. Overall, therefore, distinctiveness predicted performance very well, and any effect of norm-deviation direction must have been small compared with the size of the distinctiveness effect.

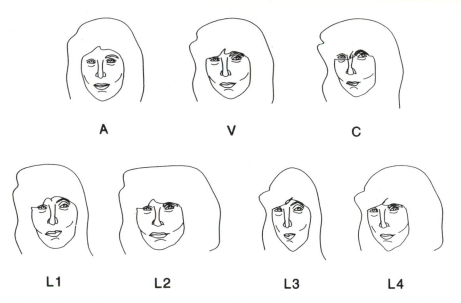

FIG. 7.2. Images of Cher used by Rhodes et al. (1996): A = anticaricature, V = veridical, C = caricature, L1, L2, L3, L4 = laterals. All distortions are 50%.

The idea that distinctiveness contributes to the power of caricatures has appealed to many theorists (J. J. Gibson, 1971; Hochberg, 1978; Rhodes et al., 1987). Nevertheless, there are reasons to be cautious about accepting distinctiveness as a complete account of that power.

First, if distinctiveness is the sole source of a caricature's power then the effectiveness of a caricature ought to depend on a face's initial distinctiveness. For example, caricatures should be more effective for faces that are not very distinctive to begin with. After all, a highly distinctive face would have few neighbours in face space with which it could be confused, and so it would gain little from being caricatured. Yet there does not seem to be a consistent relationship between a face's initial distinctiveness and the effectiveness of caricatures. Sometimes more extreme caricatures are preferred for less distinctive faces (Benson & Perrett, 1994), sometimes they are preferred for more distinctive faces, and sometimes distinctiveness does not matter (Rhodes et al., 1996 obtained each of the latter two results with different sets of faces). Nor does initial distinctiveness affect the size of the caricature advantage in face recognition (Rhodes et al., 1987; Rhodes et al., 1996), although less distinctive passerine birds appear to benefit more from caricaturing than more distinctive passerines (Rhodes & McLean, 1990). It may be possible to reconcile these diverse results with a distinctiveness account (see Rhodes et al., 1996 for detailed predictions derived from a normal density distribution of faces), but so far they seem puzzling.

Second, if caricature effects are solely distinctiveness effects, then other factors ought to influence both sorts of effect in the same way, and at least one factor does not. Inversion disrupts the recognition of typical faces (Valentine, 1991) without affecting the power of caricatures (Rhodes & Tremewan, 1994).

Third, if caricatures derive their power solely from distinctiveness, then they should not be effective for young children (< 9 years), who do not recognise distinctive faces better than more typical faces (Ellis, 1992; Johnston & Ellis, 1995). A full scale study has yet to be carried out, but pilot data (Ellis, 1992) suggest that caricatures may be effective for these children. If confirmed, these results would be difficult to reconcile with the view that caricature effects are simply distinctiveness effects.

Finally, the very notion of distinctiveness may be more complex than we have supposed. Recent results suggest that typicality (the converse of distinctiveness) has two components with independent effects on recognition (Bruce et al., 1994; Vokey & Read, 1992). One reflects familiarity (confusability with other faces) and influences false positive rates in an old/new recognition task. The other reflects memorability, and affects both hit and false alarm rates. Memorability in turn appears to reflect two components, distinctiveness of encoding and retrievability (Vokey & Read, 1992). No-one has yet explored how these factors influence individual identification (naming) of faces, but given the old/new recognition results it is not at all obvious that a single density factor will account for distinctiveness effects in identification. Distinctive faces not only lie in sparsely populated regions of face space, but they also lie far from the average face. If distinctiveness is not a unitary dimension, then perhaps distance from the norm contributes independently to distinctiveness effects in recognition, and to the power of caricatures. To test this prediction we will have to decouple the effects of density and distance from the norm, two factors that are normally highly correlated.

For these reasons it seems premature to conclude that the power of caricatures comes solely from their distinctiveness, interpreted as a density effect. It is important that we continue to investigate the power of caricatures, and that we do not rule out a role for norm-based coding at this stage.

One finding in our laterals study hinted at a role for norms in the coding of faces. In the experiment described above where subjects learned names for unfamiliar faces, we showed half the subjects norm faces (male or female, as appropriate) during learning (cf. Attneave's

1957 shape recognition study). There was a trend for exposure to the norm to facilitate subsequent recognition of caricatures and undistorted images. It is a little surprising that external presentation of norms should facilitate performance if internal norms are used anyway, but this result does suggest that explicit comparison with a norm leads to effective coding.

Although it seems clear from the laterals result that norm-deviation vectors do not define privileged directions in face space, norms might still play some role in face recognition. If so, then caricatures should only be effective when they exaggerate how faces differ from norms that we actually have. Suppose for instance that when people encounter a face from an unfamiliar race they code it using a norm based primarily on own-race faces. Then only caricatures that exaggerate how that face differs from an own-race norm should facilitate recognition. Caricatures made using objectively more appropriate, but psychologically inappropriate, other-race norms could not facilitate recognition, because they would not exaggerate the information that has been coded for those faces. Graham Byatt and I are currently testing these predictions.

CARICATURES, FACES AND EXPERTISE

At the beginning of the book I raised the question of whether caricatures exploit some special property of a face recognition system, or some more fundamental feature of recognition systems generally. The answer to this question is clear. The power of caricatures is not confined to faces, but extends to a wide variety of discriminations. Caricatures can facilitate discriminations among much simpler stimuli than faces.

In both cases, however, subjects are experts at the relevant discriminations. For faces, our expertise is the product of years of experience. For the simpler discriminations, expertise comes from extensive training in the laboratory. Might the power of caricatures therefore be a product of expertise with a class of stimuli?

Our expertise with faces is characterised by the use of relational features (Diamond & Carey, 1986; Rhodes et al., 1993) which are difficult to code in inverted faces. Therefore, if expertise is needed for caricatures to be effective, then caricatures should not be effective for inverted faces. Yet caricatures appear to be just as effective for inverted faces as for upright faces (Rhodes & Tremewan, 1995). We found this rather surprising result for several different sets of personally known and famous faces. It indicates that exaggeration of isolated features, which are available in inverted faces, can be just as effective as exaggeration of relational features for creating caricatures. It also suggests that caricature effects may not require expertise, beyond that needed to distinguish the members of a class.

The proposal that expertise is not crucial for the effectiveness of caricature leads to some interesting predictions. First, it predicts that young children, who are face novices (Carey, 1992), will find caricatures just as effective as adults. Even if they rely largely on isolated features (Carey, 1992), they should still find caricatures effective, just as adults do when faced with inverted faces that must be recognised primarily from isolated features. As already observed, pilot data suggest that young children may indeed find caricatures effective (Ellis, 1992). A second prediction is that caricatures may be effective for faces from unfamiliar races. A third prediction is that studying caricatures may help people learn to distinguish and recognise exemplars from unfamiliar homogeneous classes.

Although expertise may not be needed for caricatures to be recognisable, it may influence our perception of caricatures. In the inverted face experiments described above, caricatures were as good as undistorted images and better than anticaricatures for most sets of faces. For one set, however, caricatures were better than undistorted images, and this superportrait effect was restricted to upright faces, with which we are expert. A similar pattern was found in the experiments on bird recognition described earlier (Rhodes & McLean, 1990). Non-experts were able to recognise caricatures of birds just as well as undistorted images, but only experts recognised the caricatures better than the undistorted images. Therefore, although expertise may not be needed for caricatures to be recognised as well as undistorted images, it may be needed for them to be superportraits.

ALTERNATIVE PERSPECTIVES

Throughout this chapter I have assumed that the dimensions of face space correspond to features that can be found and measured in individual faces. It is possible, however, that the kind of features used to represent faces is quite different. Recently, the statistical technique of principal components analysis (PCA) has been applied to sets of faces to derive "features", called eigenfaces (one-dimensional arrays of pixel values) that characterise how intensity information varies between faces (for details see O'Toole et al., 1995; Turk & Pentland, 1991). Any face can be represented as a weighted sum of these eigenfaces. The eigenfaces can be displayed as faces, so that the weighted sum representing an individual face can be thought of as a composite in which the eigenface images are blended in the proportions indicated by the weights for that face.

Although eigenfaces differ from "ordinary" features in that they cannot be found on individual faces, they nevertheless define a face space in which caricatures should be effective. PCA seems to work especially well if faces are first distorted to match the average face shape, so that a vector representing each face's spatial deviation from the norm is included as part of the face's representation (Hancock, Burton, & Bruce, 1996). The subsequently derived eigenfaces then represent information about how the pattern of light and dark varies between faces. Future studies are needed to determine whether caricatures can facilitate recognition in this kind of representational system, and how exaggeration of the "distinctive" (heavily weighted) eigenfaces, and distinctive norm-deviation shape information each contribute to the power of caricatures.

The features derived using PCA are not the kind of features we are used to, but faces are still represented as sets of feature values in this approach. There, are however, quite different frameworks within which recognition can be understood. The most influential one is provided by connectionist networks, which are now widely used to model cognitive processes like recognition. Individual faces are not represented explicitly in connectionist networks as they are in the face space framework. Input patterns may be coded as values on a set of features, but faces are not stored in the network in this form. Rather, they are represented implicitly in the pattern of weights between neural-like elements that connect the input units, representing feature values, (perhaps via some hidden units) to the output units that signal recognition of a particular face. Nor does recognition of a face depend on explicit matching of inputs with stored representations. Rather, recognition occurs when stimulation from the input units spreads through the network and one of the output units is activated.

In Chapter 5 we saw that these networks can be trained to recognise visual patterns, and that caricatures can function as superportraits for these networks, just as for biological recognition systems like ourselves. But why are caricatures effective in these networks? When the networks learn to recognise objects, the strength of the connections between the input and output units is altered. The stronger the connection, the more the output unit is influenced by the activity of the input unit. In order to understand the power of caricatures, Tanaka and Simon (in press) examined the connection strengths, or "weights", between feature (input) units and face (output) units in their network. They found that the most distinctive features for each face had developed stronger connections to their corresponding face unit than the less distinctive features. It is this differential weighting of features that makes caricatures such effective representations. Apparently, the network relies more heavily on those features that discriminate best among the faces. These features are distinctive in the sense of being strongly associated with particular faces. This explanation is not restricted to faces, because although the input patterns in Tanaka and Simon's model are interpreted as faces, they are not derived from real faces, and could represent any class of patterns.

Considered in the face space framework, caricatures derive at least some of their power from their distinctiveness, either because faces with fewer neighbours are easier to recognise (the density interpretation), or because crucial norm-deviation information is more salient in faces that are further from the norm. The connectionist studies offer yet another sense in which distinctiveness may contribute to the power of caricatures. Caricatures may be effective because they exaggerate features that are strongly associated with particular faces, i.e. features that are distinctive for those faces.[12]

NOTES

1.   Walton and Bower's neonates took less than a minute to form a prototype of experienced faces, looking longer at a composite of four faces they had just seen than at a composite of four novel faces. Infants usually look longer at novel than familiar stimuli (Fantz, 1961), so if they were responding to prototypes solely in terms of their similarity to stored exemplars, then they should have looked longer at the composite of the novel faces than the composite of the familiar faces. Walton and Bower's new-borns did precisely the opposite.

2.   Little is known about the appropriate metric for calculating distance in face-space, although there is some empirical support for a Euclidean distance measure for schematic faces (Sergent, 1984b), with the distance between faces determined by the formula:

$$d_{ij} = \{\textstyle\sum |x_{im} - x_{jm}|^2\}^{1/2}, \text{ summing from } m = 1 \text{ to } M$$

where d_{ij} is the distance or dissimilarity between face i and face j, M is the dimensionality of the space, and x_{im} is the co-ordinate of stimulus i on dimension m (see Takane & Sergent, 1983 for further details).

3.   The absolute coding model described here is essentially Valentine's exemplar-only model, but the norm-based coding differs from Valentine's (1991) norm-based coding model, in which faces are represented as vectors, and some (unspecified) measure of vector similarity is used.

4.   I thank Graham Byatt for bringing this point to my attention.

5.   Interestingly, this is the case even for well-defined categories like even number (Armstrong, Gleitman, & Gleitman, 1983), suggesting that prototypes may play some role in categorization even when necessary and sufficient conditions for category membership are available.

6. A colour term is "basic" if it has one morpheme (rules out "sky-blue"), is not encompassed by the range of another colour term (rules out "scarlet" which is a kind of red), is generally applicable (rules out "blond" which only applies to hair) and is used frequently (rules out "chartreuse").

7. Not all categories have a prototype structure. Some abstract categories like rule, belief and instinct do not (Hampton, 1981). Nor do *ad hoc* categories with few shared attributes, such as the biblical categories of clean and unclean animals (Murphy & Medin, 1985).

8. On the latter view, the (unseen) prototype is familiar simply because its component features (can include attribute relationships as well as individual attributes) are familiar. The attributes are in a novel relationship in the prototype, but this may not matter, "Since the relationships between features have been seen fewer times than the features—in most experiments the exemplars are shown only once—the knowledge about relationships of features is less well stored in memory than the knowledge about features" (Solso, 1991, p.108). This argument may be plausible for artificial stimulus classes, but seems unconvincing for faces, whose relational features are more important than their component features (e.g. Carey, 1992; Rhodes et al., 1993; Young, Hellawell & Hay, 1987) and which may even be encoded holistically (Farah et al., 1995; Rhodes et al., 1987; Tanaka & Farah, 1993).

9. However, their argument rests on the erroneous assumption that similarity-to-exemplar effects are inconsistent with prototype models.

10. As illustrated in Figure 7.1 there are two possible directions for a lateral move. We constrained our laterals to reflect the bilateral symmetry of the face, by moving all the points on each side of the face the same way (either left or right, with respect to the norm-deviation direction), to give four laterals for each face.

11. In an initial study laterals were recognized less accurately than anticaricatures, a result that is difficult to reconcile with the absolute coding account of caricature effects (Carey, 1992; Carey, Rhodes, Diamond, & Hamilton, 1995). However, in that study there were some problems normalizing the images (for size and position), which appear to have made the laterals more distorted than they should have been.

12. This view is reminiscent of J.J. Gibson's (1971) suggestion that a caricature is "uniquely specific" to an individual.

CHAPTER EIGHT

The view from here

Research on the nature of caricature may ... be as central to the study of how we perceive and think about people as research on Leonardo's depth cues was central to the study of space perception.

Hochberg (1972) p.91

I began this book by raising the paradox of how caricatures can be so effective despite their obvious distortion. I also suggested that by understanding the paradox we might learn something about how recognition works, particularly recognition of objects like faces that share a configuration. I therefore set out to explore the power of caricatures in a variety of settings. This exploration has taken us through the varied terrains of art, biology, and psychology, and the time has come to see where we have ended up.

LOOKING BACK

Looking back over the journey, several conclusions emerge. First, there is little doubt that the power of caricatures, first mooted by artists in the Italian Renaissance, is considerable. Caricatures can access our memory representations of faces at least as well as undistorted images. Caricatures can sometimes be superportraits that are more like the face than the face itself. They are effective for famous faces, personally known faces, relatively unfamiliar faces, upright faces, and even inverted faces. Nor does their effectiveness seem to depend on the initial distinctiveness of the faces (see Chapter 7 for details).

Second, the power of caricatures is not confined to faces. The peak shift studies, reviewed in Chapter 5, showed that caricatures can facilitate even the simplest discriminations, between stimuli that differ on only a single dimension. Indeed, the best way to signal identity may be to display exaggerated, rather than undistorted, characteristics. Birds are the only spatially homogeneous category other than faces, that has been studied, but in that case too caricatures can facilitate recognition.

Third, the power of exaggeration seems to be fundamental to recognition systems. Humans, other animals, and computer recognition systems, all respond to the power of caricatures. As a result, caricatures have been exploited in a variety of contexts, from political satire to natural communication systems. The evolution of extreme sexual ornaments, which appeal to potential mates, provides a particularly dramatic example of how signals can exploit the power of extremes. A preference for extremes may even have shaped the evolution of human faces. For example, large chins are preferred in males (Cunningham et al., 1990), and extremes of features that distinguish attractive faces from average faces are preferred in females (Perrett et al., 1994). In general, however, average facial configurations are attractive and caricatures are not. Selection pressure for extremes may operate for traits that signal viable mates, but not for traits that signal individual identity, and there is little danger that our offspring will be caricatures of ourselves.

Fourth, no special expertise is required for caricatures to be as recognisable as undistorted images. Some experience may be needed to distinguish the members of a homogeneous class (or perhaps to abstract a norm for the class), but the kind of expertise that takes years to develop is not needed to recognise caricatures. Nevertheless, expertise may be needed for caricatures to be superportraits. Caricatures seem to be superportraits for bird experts, but not for non-experts, and for face experts (ordinary adults), when viewing upright faces but not inverted faces with which they lack expertise (see Chapter 7 for details).

Turning to the question of how caricatures can be so effective, I have suggested that the answer will depend on what kind of representational system is used. If some form of norm-based coding is used, then caricatures will be effective because they highlight the way that each exemplar differs from the norm. If stimuli are coded as absolute values on some set of relevant dimensions, then caricatures may derive their power from their location in sparsely populated regions of the stimulus space. Alternatively, caricatures may be effective because they exaggerate features that are strongly or uniquely associated with particular faces.

Norm-based coding provides an ideal solution to the homogeneity problem, and we have seen that it is used to represent many simple unidimensional stimuli. Moreover, people certainly seem to abstract norms for a variety of natural and artificial classes, as they must if norms are to play a role in representing the members of those classes. Therefore, in at least some cases, caricatures may derive their power from exaggerating how exemplars differ from a norm.

But what about the case of faces? The question of exactly what role, if any, norms play in coding faces is far from resolved. Until it is, we will not have a complete account of why caricatures are such effective representations of faces. In the meantime, however, I offer two conclusions about the power of face caricatures, which do not depend on resolving the coding issue. First, these caricatures do not derive their power from resemblance to caricatured traces in long-term memory. If they did, then they should only facilitate recognition for familiar faces, and this is not the case. Second, distinctiveness, in some sense, contributes to the power of caricatures. The question of whether it is distinctiveness in the sense of distance from other faces in face space, or distinctiveness in the sense of distance from the norm that is crucial remains to be resolved, along with the broader issue of how faces are mentally represented.

LOOKING FORWARD

The challenge now is to test more detailed models of how faces are mentally represented. In particular, we must resolve what role, if any, norms play in coding faces. The difficulties associated with distinguishing prototype models from exemplar-only models of categorisation (see Chapter 7), and in sorting out questions about the nature of mental representations generally (Anderson, 1978; Kosslyn & Pomerantz, 1977), suggest that this will not be an easy challenge to meet. Too narrow a focus on this issue may therefore be unwise.

Attention should also be given to other issues, such as the role of expertise in caricature recognition. The available data suggest that expertise may be needed for caricatures to be superportraits, but not for caricatures to be as recognisable as undistorted images. However, the performance of experts and non-experts has never been compared for the same stimuli. The apparent restriction of superportrait effects to experts may therefore be due to the use of more homogeneous stimuli for those subjects. For example, the bird experts in our study (Rhodes & McLean, 1990) had to identify passerine birds, which are very similar in shape, whereas the non-experts identified birds from a more heterogeneous set (duck, kiwi, ostrich, etc.). Future studies should compare the performance of experts and non-experts on the same stimuli. Homogeneous classes other than birds and faces should also be studied.

Other questions also remain to be answered. How many face-spaces, or norms, do we actually have, and how are they acquired? Are they solely the result of experience, or has evolution equipped us with an initial face-space, or an initial norm? Perhaps norm-based coding is part of our innate endowment, and expertise allows a richer and more complex set of dimensions to be represented in the norm (see Carey & Diamond, 1994). Another question concerning the development of expertise, is how much experience we need with a structurally distinct class of faces, such as those from an unfamiliar race, before we develop separate face-spaces and/or norms. These are open questions, but ones that we have the tools to answer. For example, we could learn a lot about the face-spaces and/or norms that people use, and how they develop with age and experience, by studying the effectiveness of caricatures created using different norms. The closer the norms are to the centre of psychological face-space, and the more closely the dimensions manipulated match those represented in face-space, the better the caricatures should be.

The members of a homogeneous class such as faces share a configuration and are distinguished by variations within that configuration. Whether or not those variations are identified by comparison with a norm, questions remain about how these distinctive variations are represented in memory. Are they coded as lists of values on some set of dimensions on which faces vary, or are they represented more holistically (Farah et al., 1995; Rhodes et al., 1987)? Do we recognise faces by comparing their values on each relevant dimension with those of our memory representations? Or do we use some more holistic process?

On a more pragmatic note, caricatures may have considerable potential as a forensic tool. We have seen that line drawing caricatures can be identified better than undistorted images, even if the faces are relatively unfamiliar, and that caricatures of novel faces can be readily rejected as unfamiliar. The forensic implications would be especially exciting if photographic caricatures prove to be equally effective. Commercially available morphing programs could then be used to caricature mug-shot photographs for presentation to witnesses. Even if superportrait effects are confined to simpler line drawing images, caricatures might still be useful when photographs of suspects are not available. In that case, caricatures of Identikit-style constructions based on witnesses' descriptions could be used. A word of caution though; caricatures seem to be more effective for some faces than others and we currently have little idea about what accounts for this variability. The most obvious hypothesis, that the effectiveness of caricaturing depends on how distinctive a face is to begin with, has received little empirical support.

For many objects there is no need to represent subtle metric differences in a shared configuration. They can be recognised using a simpler system that codes the object's parts and/or the spatial arrangement of those parts (e.g. Biederman, 1987, 1990, 1995; Cave & Kosslyn, 1993; Marr, 1982). Therefore, to get a complete picture of how recognition works, we need to know how these two recognition systems fit together in the architecture of cognition. Are they independent systems, as some have suggested (Corballis, 1991; Farah, 1992, 1995)? Or do they work in a more co-operative spirit, with an initial part-based representation signalling the presence of a face and recruiting an appropriate norm for the more subtle coding needed to recognise a favourite aunt, an old friend, or a workmate?

In addition to suggesting a potential solution to the homogeneity problem, the power of caricatures offers an important insight into the nature of representation more generally. It reinforces Gombrich's point that a successful representation need not resemble or mimic what it represents. What it must do, is elicit in us an *equivalent response* to that elicited by what it represents. From this perspective, psychologists and artists are engaged in a similar quest. Each must discover how to trigger the desired response, the artist in order to create a convincing likeness, and the psychologist in order to understand the crucial features for recognition. With the invention of caricature, artists discovered a powerful technique for eliciting equivalent, or even enhanced responses. They also provided psychologists with a powerful tool for studying recognition.

References

Alba, J.W., & Hasher, L. (1983). Is memory schematic? *Psychological Bulletin, 93*, 203–231.

Alley, T.R., & Cunningham, M.R. (1991). Averaged faces are attractive, but very attractive faces are not average. *Psychological Science, 2*, 123–125.

Alley, T.R., & Hildebrandt, K.A. (1988). Determinants and consequences of facial aesthetics. In T.R. Alley (Ed.), *Social and applied aspects of perceiving faces*. Hillsdale, NJ: Lawrence Erlbaum Associates Inc.

Anderson, J.R. (1978). Arguments concerning representations for mental imagery. *Psychological Review, 85*, 249–277.

Andersson, M. (1982). Female choice selects for extreme tail length in a widowbird. *Nature, 299*, 818–820.

Andersson, M. (1994). *Sexual selection*. Princeton, NJ: Princeton University Press.

Antal, F. (1962). *Hogarth and his place in European art*. New York: Basic Books.

Arak, A., & Enquist, M. (1993). Hidden preferences and signal evolution. *Philosophical Proceedings of the Royal Society of London, Series B, 340*, 207–213.

Armstrong, S.L., Gleitman, L.R., & Gleitman, H. (1983). What some concepts might not be. *Cognitive Psychology, 13*, 263–308.

Attneave, F. (1954). Some informational aspects of visual perception. *Psychological Review, 61*, 183–193.

Attneave, F. (1957). Transfer of experience with a class-schema to identification-learning of patterns and shapes. *Journal of Experimental Psychology, 54*, 81–88.

Baerends, G.P. (1982). Supernormality. *Behaviour, 82*, 358–363.

Baerends, G.P., & Kruijt, J.P. (1973). Stimulus selection. In R.A. Hinde & J. Stevenson-Hinde (Eds.), *Constraints on learning: Limitations and predispositions* (pp.23–50). New York: Academic Press.

Balmford, A., Thomas, A.L.R., & Jones, I.L. (1993). Aerodynamics and the evolution of long tails in birds. *Nature, 361*, 628–631.

Baltrusaitis, J. (1989). *Abberations: An essay on the legend of forms.* Cambridge, MA: MIT Press.

Barash, D.P. (1982). *Sociobiology and behaviour.* New York: Elsevier North Holland.

Barrett, S.C.H. (1987). Mimicry in plants. *Scientific American, 257*, 68–75.

Barsalou, L.W. (1985). Ideals, central tendency, and frequency of instantiation as determinants of graded structure in categories. *Journal of Experimental Psychology: Learning, Memory, & Cognition, 11*, 629–654.

Bartlett, F.C. (1932). *Remembering: A study in experimental and social psychology.* Cambridge: Cambridge University Press.

Bartlett, J.C. (1994, February). Inversion and configuration of faces. In J.Bartlett (Chair), *Face recognition by computers and people.* Symposium at the meeting of the American Academy for the Advancement of Science, San Francisco.

Bartlett, J.C., Hurry, S., & Thorley, W. (1984). Typicality and familiarity of faces. *Memory & Cognition, 12*, 219–228.

Bartlett, J.C., & Searcy, J. (1993). Inversion and configuration of faces. *Cognitive Psychology, 25*, 281–316.

Basolo, A. (1990a). Female preference predates the evolution of the sword in swordtail fish. *Science, 250*, 808–810.

Basolo, A. (1990b). Female preferences for male sword length in the green swordtail, *Xiphophorus helleri* (Pisces: Poeciliidae). *Animal Behaviour, 40*, 332–338.

Bateson, P. (Ed.) (1983). *Mate choice.* Cambridge: Cambridge University Press.

Battig, W.F., & Montague, W.E. (1969). Category norms for verbal items in 56 categories. *Journal of Experimental Psychology Monograph, 80*, 1–46.

Benson, P.J. (1995). *Recognition of famous-face photographic-quality caricatures from their internal facial features.* Unpublished manuscript, Oxford University.

Benson, P.J., & Perrett, D.I. (1991a). Synthesising continuous-tone caricatures. *Image & Vision Computing, 9*, 123–129.

Benson, P.J., & Perrett, D.I. (1991b). Gregorian physiognomy. *Perception, 20*, 279.

Benson, P.J., & Perrett, D.I. (1991c). Perception and recognition of photographic quality facial caricatures: Implications for the recognition of natural images. *European Journal of Cognitive Psychology, 3*, 105–135.

Benson, P.J., & Perrett, D.I. (1992). Face to face with the perfect image. *New Scientist*, Feb 22, No 1809, 26–29.

Benson, P.J., & Perrett, D.I. (1994). Visual processing of facial distinctiveness. *Perception, 23*, 75–93.

Benson, P.J., Perrett, D.I., & Davis, D.N. (1989). Towards a quantitative understanding of facial caricatures. In V. Bruce & M. Burton (Eds.), *Processing images of faces* (pp.69–87). NJ: Ablex.

Berlin, B., & Kay, P. (1969). *Basic color terms: Their universality and evolution.* Berkeley: University of California Press.

Berry, D.S., & Zebrowitz-McArthur, L. (1988). The impact of age-related craniofacial changes on social perception. In T.R. Alley (Ed.), *Social and applied aspects of perceiving faces* (pp.63–87). Hillsdale, NJ: Lawrence Erlbaum Associates Inc.

Biederman, I. (1987). Recognition-by-components: A theory of human image understanding. *Psychological Review, 94*, 115–147.

Biederman, I. (1990). Higher-level vision. In D.N. Osherson, S. Kosslyn, & J. Hollerbach (Eds.), *An invitation to cognitive science: Visual cognition and action, Vol 2* (pp.41–72). Cambridge, MA: MIT Press.

Biederman, I. (1995). Visual object recognition. In S.M. Kosslyn & D.N. Osherson (Eds.), *An invitation to cognitive science: Visual Cognition, Vol. 2* (pp.121–165). Cambridge, MA: MIT Press.

Biederman, I., & Gerhardstein, P.C. (1993). Recognizing depth-rotated objects: Evidence and conditions for three-dimensional viewpoint invariance. *Journal of Experimental Psychology: Human Perception & Performance, 19*, 1162–1182.

Biederman, I., & Gerhardstein, P.C. (1995). Viewpoint-dependent mechanisms in visual object recognition: Reply to Tarr & Bülthoff (1995). *Journal of Experimental Psychology: Human Perception & Performance, 21*, 1506–1514.

Biederman, I., & Ju, G. (1988). Surface versus edge-based determinants of visual recognition. *Cognitive Psychology, 20*, 38–64.

Bolhuis, J.J., De Vos, G.J., & Kruijt, J.P. (1990). Filial imprinting and associative learning. *Quarterly Journal of Experimental Psychology, 42B*, 313–329.

Borgia, G. (1986). Sexual selection in bower birds. *Scientific American, 254*, 92–100.

Bothwell, R.K., Brigham, J.C., & Malpass, R.S. (1989). Cross-racial identification. *Personality & Social Psychology Bulletin, 15*, 19–25.

Bradbury, J.W., & Andersson, M.B. (Eds.). (1987). *Sexual selection: Testing the alternatives*. Chichester: Wiley.

Brennan, S.E. (1982). *Caricature generator*. Unpublished Master's thesis. MIT, Cambridge, MA.

Brennan, S.E. (1985). The caricature generator. *Leonardo, 18*, 170–178.

Brooks, M., & Pomiankowski, A. (1994). Symmetry is in the eye of the beholder. *Trends in Ecology & Evolution, 9*, 201–202.

Bruce, V., Burton, M.A., & Dench, N. (1994). What's distinctive about a distinctive face? *Quarterly Journal of Experimental Psychology, 47A*, 119–141.

Bruce, V., Doyle, T., Dench, N., & Burton, M. (1991). Remembering facial configurations. *Cognition, 38*, 109–144.

Bruce, V., Hanna, E., Dench, N., Healey, P., & Burton, M. (1992). The importance of "mass" in line drawings of faces. *Applied Cognitive Psychology, 6*, 619–628.

Bruce, V., Healey, P., Burton, M., Doyle, T., Coombes, A., & Linney, A. (1991). Recognising facial surfaces. *Perception, 20*, 755–769.

Brunas-Wagstaff, J., Young, A.W., & Ellis, A.W. (1992). Repetition priming follows spontaneous but not prompted recognition of familiar faces. *Quarterly Journal of Psychology, 44A*, 423–454.

Burley, N. (1986). Sexual selection for aesthetic traits in species with parental care. *American Naturalist, 127*, 415–445.

Carey, S. (1992). Becoming a face expert. *Philosophical Transactions of the Royal Society of London, Series B, 335*, 95–103.

Carey, S., & Diamond, R. (1977). From piecemeal to configurational representation of faces. *Science, 195*, 312–314.

Carey, S., & Diamond, R. (1994). Are faces perceived as configurations more by adults than by children? *Visual Cognition, 1*, 253–274.

Carey, S., Rhodes, G., Diamond, R., & Hamilton, J. (1995). *Norm-based coding of faces: Evidence from studies of caricature recognition.* Unpublished manuscript, Massachusetts Institute of Technology.

Carroll, L. (1946). *Through the looking glass and what Alice found there.* New York: Random House.

Cave, C.B., & Kosslyn, S.M. (1993). The role of parts and spatial relations in object identification. *Perception, 22*, 229–248.

Chilvers, I., Osborne, H., & Farr, D. (1988). *The Oxford dictionary of art.* Oxford: Oxford University Press.

Chiroro, P., & Valentine, T. (1995). An investigation of the contact hypothesis of the own-race bias in face recognition. *Quarterly Journal of Experimental Psychology, 48A*, 879–894.

Cohen, M.E., & Carr, W.J. (1975). Facial recognition and the von Restorff effect. *Bulletin of the Psychonomic Society, 6*, 383–384.

Concar, D. (1995). Sex and the symmetrical body. *New Scientist, 146*, 40–44.

Corballis, M.C. (1988). Recognition of disoriented shapes. *Psychological Review, 95*, 115–123.

Corballis, M.C. (1991). *The lopsided ape: The evolution of the generative mind.* New York: Oxford University Press.

Cowling, M. (1989). *The artist as anthropologist: The representation of type and character in Victorian art.* Cambridge: Cambridge University Press.

Crocker, G., & Day, T. (1987). An advantage to mate choice in the seaweed fly, *Coelopa figida. Behavioral Ecology & Sociobiology, 20*, 295–301.

Cronin, H. (1991). *The ant and the peacock: Altruism and sexual selection from Darwin to today.* Cambridge University Press: Cambridge.

Cummins, R. (1989). *Meaning and mental representation.* Cambridge, MA: Bradford Book, MIT Press.

Cunningham, M.R. (1986). Measuring the physical in physical attractiveness: Quasi-experiments on the sociobiology of female facial beauty. *Journal of Personality & Social Psychology, 50*, 925–935.

Cunningham, M.R., Barbee, A.P., & Pike, C.L. (1990). What do women want? Facialmetric assessment of multiple motives in the perception of male facial physical attractiveness. *Journal of Personality & Social Psychology, 59*, 61–72.

Damasio, A.R., Tranel, D., & Damasio, H. (1990). Face agnosia and the neural substrates of memory. *Annual Review of Neuroscience, 13*, 89–109.

Darwin, C.R. (1871). *The descent of man and selection in relation to sex.* London: John Murray.

Darwin, F. (Ed). (1887). *The life and letters of Charles Darwin.* London: John Murray.

Davidoff, J.B. (1986). The specificity of face perception: Evidence from psychological investigations. In R. Bruyer (Ed.), *The neuropsychology of facial perception and facial expression.* Hillsdale, NJ: Lawrence Erlbaum Associates Inc.

Davies, G., Ellis, H., & Shepherd, J. (1978). Face recognition accuracy as a function of mode of representation. *Journal of Applied Psychology, 63*, 383–384.

Dawkins, M.S. (1993). Are there general principles of signal design? *Philosophical Transactions of the Royal Society of London, Series B, 340*, 251–255.

de Renzi, E. (1986). Current issues in prosopagnosia. In H.D. Ellis, M.A. Jeeves, F. Newcombe, & A. Young (Eds.). *Aspects of face processing.* Dordrecht: Martinus Nijhoff.

della Porta, G. (1586). *De Humana Physiognomia.* Naples.

Dewdney, A.K. (1986). Computer recreations: The compleat computer caricaturist and a whimsical tour of face space. *Scientific American, 255*, 20–28.

Diamond, R., & Carey, S. (1986). Why faces are and are not special: An effect of expertise. *Journal of Experimental Psychology: General, 115*, 107–117.

Dobzhansky, T. (1970). *Genetics of the evolutionary process.* New York: Columbia University Press.

Domjan, M., & Burkhard, B. (1986). *The principles of learning and behavior (2nd ed.).* Monterey, CA: Brooks/Cole Publishing.

Eberhard, W.G. (1990). Animal genitalia and female choice. *American Scientist, 78*, 134–141.

Elio, R., & Anderson, J.R. (1981). The effects of category generalizations and instance similarity on schema abstraction. *Journal of Experimental Psychology: Human Learning & Memory, 7*, 397–417.

Ellis, H.D. (1990). Developmental trends in face recognition. *The Psychologist, 3*, 114–119.

Ellis, H.D. (1992). The development of face processing skills. *Philosophical Transactions of the Royal Society of London, Series B, 335*, 105–111.

Ellis, H.D., Shepherd, J.W., & Davies, G.M. (1979). Identification of familiar and unfamiliar faces from internal and external features: Some implications for theories of face recognition. *Perception, 8*, 431–439.

Ellis, H.D., Shepherd, J.W., Gibling, F., & Shepherd, J. (1988). Stimulus factors in face learning. In M.M. Gruneberg, P.E. Morris, & R.N. Sykes (Eds.), *Practical aspects of memory: Current research and issues, Vol 1: Memory in everyday life* (pp.136–143). Chichester: Wiley.

Ellis, H.D., & Young, A.W. (1989). Are faces special? In A.W. Young & H.D. Ellis (Eds.), *Handbook of research on face processing* (pp. 1–26). Amsterdam; North-Holland.

Encyclopedia of world art. (1960). New York: McGraw-Hill.

Endler, J.A. (1992). Signals, signal conditions, and the direction of evolution. *The American Naturalist, 139*, S125–S153.

Engelhard, G., Foster, S.P., & Day, T.H. (1989). Genetic differences in mating success and female choice in seaweed flies (*Coeloa frigida*). *Heredity, 62*, 123–131.

Enquist, M., & Arak, A. (1993). Selection of exaggerated male traits by female aesthetic senses. *Nature, 361*, 446–448.

Enquist, M., & Arak, A. (1994. Symmetry, beauty and evolution. *Nature, 372*, 169–172.

Estes, W.K. (1986). Memory storage and retrieval processes in category learning. *Journal of Experimental Psychology: General, 115*, 155–174.

Etcoff, N.L. (1994). Beauty and the beholder. *Nature, 368*, 186–187.

Eysenck, M.W., & Keane, M.T. (1990). *Cognitive psychology: A student's handbook*. Hove, UK: Lawrence Erlbaum Associates Ltd.

Fantz, R.L. (1961). The origin of form perception. *Scientific American, 202*, 66–72.

Farah, M. (1990). *Visual agnosia: Disorders of object recognition and what they tell us about normal vision*. Cambridge, MA: MIT Press.

Farah, M.J. (1992). Is an object an object an object? Cognitive and neuropsychological investigations of domain specificity in visual object recognition. *Current Directions in Psychological Science, 1*, 164–169.

Farah, M.J., (1995). Dissociable systems for recognition: A cognitive neuropsychology approach. In S.M. Kosslyn & D.N. Osherson (Eds.), *An invitation to cognitive science: Visual cognition, Vol. 2* (pp.101–119). Cambridge, MA: MIT Press.

Farah, M.J., Tanaka, J.W., & Drain, H.M. (1995). What causes the face inversion effect? *Journal of Experimental Psychology: Human Perception & Performance, 21*, 3, 628–634.

Fisher, R.A. (1915). The evolution of sexual preference. *Eugenics Review, 7*, 184–192.

Fisher, R.A. (1930). *The genetical theory of natural selection*. Oxford: Clarendon Press.

Franks, J.J., & Bransford, J.D. (1971). Abstraction of visual patterns. *Journal of Experimental Psychology, 90*, 65–74.

Frege, G. (1952). On sense and reference. In P. Geach & M. Black (Eds.), *Translations from the philosophical writings of Gottlieb Frege*. Oxford: Basil Blackwell.

Galton, F. (1878). Composite portraits. *Journal of the Anthropological Institute of Great Britain and Ireland, 8*, 132–142.

Galton, F. (1883). *Inquiries into human faculty and its development*. London: Macmillan & Co.

Gardner, B.T., & Wallach, L. (1965). Shapes of figures identified as a baby's head. *Perceptual & Motor Skills, 20*, 135–142.

Geipel, J. (1972). *The cartoon: A short history of graphic comedy and satire*. Trowbridge & London: David & Charles Publishers Ltd.

Gibson, E.J. (1969). *Principles of perceptual learning and development*. New York: Appleton-Century-Croft.

Gibson, J.J. (1947). *Motion picture testing and research*. Report No. 7, AAF Aviation Psychology Research Reports. Washington, U.S. Gov. Printing Office.

Gibson, J.J. (1971). The information available in pictures. *Leonardo, 4*, 27–35.

Gluck, M.A., & Bower, G.H. (1988). From conditioning to category learning: An adaptive network model. *Journal of Experimental Psychology: General, 117*, 227–247.

Going, M., & Read, J.D. (1974). Effects of uniqueness, sex of subject, and sex of photograph on facial recognition. *Perceptual & Motor Skills, 39*, 109–110.

Goldstein, A.G., & Chance, J.E. (1980). Memory for faces and schema theory. *Journal of Psychology, 105*, 47–59.

Gombrich, E.H. (1960). *Art and illusion: A study in the psychology of pictorial representation*. New York: Pantheon Press.

Gombrich, E.H. (1963). The cartoonist's armory. *South Atlantic Quarterly, 17*, 189–228.

Gombrich, E.H. (1972). The mask and the face: the perception of physiognomic likeness in life and in art. In E.H. Gombrich, J. Hochberg, & M. Black, *Art, perception and reality* (pp.1–46). Baltimore & London: The Johns Hopkins University Press.

Gombrich, E.H., & Kris, E. (1940). *Caricature*. Harmondsworth: Penguin Books Ltd.

Gombrich, E.H., & Kris, E. (1952). The principles of caricature. In E. Kris, *Psychoanalytic explorations in art* (pp.189–203). New York: International Universities press.

Gordon, I.E., (1989). *Theories of visual perception*. Chichester: John Wiley & Sons.

Goren, C.C., Sarty, M., & Wu, P.Y.K. (1975). Visual following and pattern discrimination of face-like stimuli by newborn infants. *Pediatrics, 56,* 544–549.

Gould, J. L., & Gould, C. G. (1989). *Sexual selection*. New York: Scientific American Library, W.H. Freeman.

Grammer, K., & Thornhill, R. (1994). Human (*Homo sapiens*) facial attractiveness and sexual selection: The role of symmetry and averageness. *Journal of Comparative Psychology, 108,* 233–242.

Grofman, B. (1989). Richard Nixon as Pinocchio, Richard II, and Santa Claus: The use of allusion in political satire. *Journal of Politics, 51,* 165–173.

Guilford, T., & Dawkins, M. (1991). Receiver psychology and the evolution of animal signals. *Animal Behaviour, 42,* 1–14.

Guilford, T., & Dawkins, M. (1993). Receiver psychology and the design of animal signals. *Trends in Neurosciences, 16,* 430–436.

Hagen, M.A., & Perkins, D. (1983). A refutation of the superfidelity of caricatures relative to photographs. *Perception, 12,* 55–61.

Haig, N.D. (1984). The effect of feature displacement on face recognition. *Perception, 13,* 505–512.

Haig, N.D. (1985). How faces differ: A new comparative technique. *Perception, 14,* 601–615.

Halliday, T.R. (1978). Sexual selection and mate choice. In J.R. Krebs & N.B. Davies (Eds.), *Behavioural ecology: An evolutionary approach* (pp.180–213). Oxford: Blackwell.

Hamilton, W.D., & Zuk, M. (1982). Heritable true fitness and bright birds: A role for parasites? *Science, 218,* 384–387.

Hammond, B. (1988). *The New Zealand encyclopaedia of fly fishing*. Auckland: Halcyon Press.

Hampton, J. (1981). An investigation of the nature of abstract concepts. Memory & Cognition, 9, 149–156.

Hampton, J. (1993). Prototype models of concept representation. In I. van Mechelen, J. Hampton, R.S. Michalski, & P. Theuns (Eds.), *Categories and concepts: Theoretical views and inductive data analysis*. London: Academic Press.

Hancock, P.J., Burton, A.M., & Bruce, V. (1996). Face processing: Human perception and principal components analysis. *Memory & Cognition, 24,* 26–40.

Hanson, H.M. (1959). Effect of discrimination training on stimulus generalization. *Journal of Experimental Psychology, 58,* 321–334.

Harvey, P.H., & Bradbury, J.W. (1991). Sexual selection. In J.R. Krebs & N.B. Davies (Eds.), *Behavioural ecology: An evolutionary approach* (3rd ed.) (pp.203–233). Oxford: Blackwell.

Head, H. (1920). *Studies in Neurology, Vol II.* London: Hodder & Stoughton and Oxford University Press.

Hebb, D.O. (1949). *The organisation of behaviour.* New York: Wiley.

Hebb, D.O., & Foord, E.N. (1945). Errors of visual recognition and the nature of the trace. *Journal of Experimental Psychology, 35,* 335–348.

Helson, H. (1947). Adaptation-level as frame of reference for prediction of psychophysical data. *American Journal of Psychology, 60,* 1–29.

Helson, H. (1964). *Adaptation level theory.* New York: Harper & Row.

Hildreth, E.C., & Ullman, S. (1989). The computational study of vision. In M.I. Posner (Ed.), *Foundations of cognitive science* (pp.581–630). Cambridge, MA: MIT Press.

Hillier, B. (1970). *Cartoons and caricatures.* London: Studio Vista Ltd/Dutton Pictureback.

Hintzman, D.L. (1986). "Schema abstraction" in a multiple-trace memory model. *Psychological Review, 93,* 411–428.

Hintzman, D.L., & Ludlum, G. (1980). Differential forgetting of prototypes and old instances: Simulation by an exemplar-based classification model. *Memory & Cognition, 8,* 378–382.

Hochberg, J. (1972). The representation of things and people. In E.H. Gombrich, J. Hochberg, & M. Black, *Art, perception and reality* (pp.47–94). Baltimore & London: The Johns Hopkins University Press.

Hochberg, J.E. (1978). *Perception (2nd ed.).* Englewood Cliffs, NJ: Prentice-Hall.

Hoffman, D.D., & Richards, W.A. (1984). Parts of recognition. In S. Pinker (Ed.), *Visual cognition* (pp.65–96). Cambridge, MA: MIT Press.

Hogan, J.A., Kruijt, J.P., & Frijlink, J.H. (1975). Supernormality in a learning situation. *Zeitschrift für Tierpsychologie, 38,* 212–218.

Höglund, J., Eriksson, M., & Lindell, L.E. (1990). Females of the lek-breeding great snipe, *Gallinago media,* prefer males with white tails. *Animal Behaviour, 40,* 23–32.

Homa, D., Goldhardt, B., Burruel-Homa, L., & Carson Smith, J. (1993). Influence of manipulated category knowledge on prototype classification and recognition. *Memory & Cognition, 21,* 529–538.

Homa, D., Sterling, S., & Trepel, L. (1981). Limitations of exemplar-based generalization and the abstraction of categorical information. *Journal of Experimental Psychology: Human Learning & Memory, 7,* 418–439.

Honig, W.K., & Urcuioli, P.J. (1981). The legacy of Guttman and Kalish (1956): 25 years of research on stimulus generalization. *Journal of the Experimental Analysis of Behavior, 36,* 405–445.

Horn, M. (Ed.) (1980). *The world encyclopedia of cartoons.* New York: Gale Research Co., Chelsea House Publishers.

Inglis, I.R., & Isaacson, A.J. (1984). The response of woodpigeons (*Columba Palumbus*) to pigeon decoys in various postures: A quest for a super-normal alarm stimulus. *Behaviour, 90,* 224–250.

Inn, D., Walden, K.J., & Solso, R.L. (1993). Facial prototype formation in children. *Bulletin of the Psychonomic Society, 31,* 197–200.

Johnson, M.H., Dziurawiec, S., Ellis, H., & Morton, J. (1991). Newborns' preferential tracking of face-like stimuli and its subsequent decline. *Cognition, 40,* 1–19.

Johnson, M.H., & Morton, J. (1991). *Biology and cognitive development: The case of face recognition.* Oxford: Blackwell.

Johnston, R.A., & Ellis, H.D. (1995). Age effects in the processing of typical and distinctive faces. *Quarterly Journal of Experimental Psychology, 48A*, 447–465.

Johnstone, R.A. (1994). Female preference for symmetrical males as a by-product of selection for mate recognition. *Nature, 372*, 172–175.

Jolicoeur, P. (1985). The time to name disoriented natural objects. *Memory & Cognition, 13*, 289–303.

Jolicoeur, P. (1990). Identification of disoriented objects: A dual systems theory. *Mind & Language, 5*, 387–410.

Koenderink, J.J., & Van Doorn, A.J. (1979). The internal representation of solid shape with respect to vision. *Biological Cybernetics, 32*, 211–216.

Kirkpatrick, M., & Ryan, M.J. (1991). The evolution of mating preferences and the paradox of the lek. *Nature, 350*, 33–38.

Koffka, K. (1935). *Principles of Gestalt Psychology*. New York: Harcourt, Brace.

Köhler, W. (1939). Simple structural functions in the chimpanzee and in the chicken. In W.D. Ellis (Ed.), *A source book of Gestalt Psychology* (pp. 217–227). New York: Harcourt, Brace.

Kosslyn, S.M., & Pomerantz, J.R. (1977). Imagery, propositions, and the form of internal representations. *Cognitive Psychology, 9*, 52–76.

Krebs, J.R. (1991). Animal communication: Ideas derived from Tinbergen's activities. In M.S. Dawkins, T.R. Halliday, & R. Dawkins (Eds.), *The Tinbergen legacy*. London: Chapman & Hall.

Lane, W.C., & Browne, N.E. (1906). *A.L.A. Portrait Index*. Washington, DC: Government Printing Office.

Langlois, J.H., & Roggman, L.A. (1990). Attractive faces are only average. *Psychological Science, 1*, 115–121.

Langlois, J.H., Roggman, L.A., Casey, R.J., Ritter, J.M., Rieser-Danner, L.A., & Jenkins, V.Y. (1987). Infant preferences for attractive faces: Rudiments of a stereotype? *Developmental Psychology, 23*, 363–369.

Langlois, J.H., Roggman, L.A., & Musselman, L. (1994). What is average and what is not average about attractive faces? *Psychological Science, 5*, 214–220.

Lavater, J.C. (1789). *Essay on physiognomy for the promotion of the knowledge and the love of mankind*. London: John Murray.

Lavin, D. (1988). *Recognizing profile silhouettes: An investigation of the internal representation of familiar faces*. Unpublished doctoral dissertation, Stanford University, Stanford, CA.

le Brun, C. (1702). *Méthode pour apprendre à deviner les passions*. Amsterdam: F. van der Plaats.

Levine, S.C. (1989). The question of faces: Special is in the brain of the beholder. In A.W. Young & H.D. Ellis (Eds.), *Handbook of research on face processing* (pp.37–48). Amsterdam: North-Holland.

Light, L.L., Kayra-Stuart, F., & Hollander, S. (1979). Recognition memory for typical and unusual faces. *Journal of Experimental Psychology: Human Learning & Memory, 5*, 212–219.

Lucie-Smith, E. (1981). *The art of caricature*. Ithaca, NY: Cornell University Press.

MacLaury, R.E. (1991). Prototypes revisited. *Annual Review of Anthropology, 20*, 55–74.

Maier, R.A., Holmes, D.L., Slaymaker, F.L., & Reich, J.N. (1984). The perceived attractiveness of preterm infants. *Infant Behavior & Development, 7*, 403–414.

Majerus, M. (1986). The genetics and evolution of female choice. *Trends in Ecology & Evolution, 1*, 1–7.

Malt, B.C. (1989). An on-line investigation of prototype and exemplar strategies in classification. *Journal of Experimental Psychology: Learning, Memory & Cognition, 15*, 539–555.

Marler, P., & Hamilton, W.J. III (1966). *Mechanisms of Animal Behavior*. New York: Wiley.

Marr, D. (1982). *Vision*. San Francisco: Freeman.

Mauro, R., & Kubovy, M. (1992). Caricature and face recognition. *Memory & Cognition, 20*, 433–440.

McCabe, V. (1988). Facial proportions, perceived age, and caregiving. In T.R. Alley (Ed.), *Social and applied aspects of perceiving faces* (pp.89–95). Hillsdale, NJ: Lawrence Erlbaum Associates Inc.

McClelland, J.L., & Rumelhart, D.E. (1985). Distributed memory and the representation of general and specific information. *Journal of Experimental Psychology: General, 114*, 159–188.

McClelland, J.L., Rumelhart, D.E., & the PDP Research Group. (1986). *Parallel distributed processing: Explorations in the microstructure of cognition, Volume 1: Foundations*. Cambridge, MA: MIT Press, A Bradford Book.

McLean, I.G., & Rhodes, G. (1991). Enemy recognition in birds. In D.M. Power (Ed.). *Current ornithology: Vol 8*. New York: Plenum Press.

McLean, I.G., & Waas, J.R. (1987). Do cuckoo chicks mimic the begging calls of their hosts? *Animal Behaviour, 35*, 1896–1898.

Meadows, J.C. (1974). The anatomical basis of prosopagnosia. *Journal of Neurology, Neurosurgery & Psychiatry, 37*, 489–501.

Medin, D.L. (1986). Comment on "Memory storage and retrieval processes in category learning". *Journal of Experimental Psychology: General, 115*, 373–381.

Medin, D.L., Altom, M.W., & Murphy, T.D. (1984). Given vs. induced category representations: Use of prototype and exemplar information in classification. *Journal of Experimental Psychology: Learning, Memory & Cognition, 10*, 333–352.

Medin, D.L., & Florian, J.E. (1992). Abstraction and selective coding in exemplar-based models of categorization. In A.F. Healy, S.M. Kosslyn, & R.M. Shiffrin (Eds.), *From learning processes to cognitive processes: Essays in honor of William K. Estes*. Hillsdale, NJ: Lawrence Erlbaum Associates Inc.

Medin, D.L., & Schaffer, M.M. (1978). A context theory of classification learning. *Psychological Review, 85*, 207–238.

Medin, D.L., & Smith, E.E. (1984). Concepts and concept formation. *Annual Review of Psychology, 35*, 113–138.

Mervis, C., Catlin, J., & Rosch, E. (1976). Relationships among goodness-of-example, category norms, and word frequency. *Bulletin of the Psychonomic Society, 7*, 283–284.

Meyer, A., Morrissey, J.M., & Scharti, M. (1994). Recurrent origin of a sexually selected trait in *Xiphophorus* fishes inferred from a molecular phylogeny. *Nature, 368*, 539–542.

Møller, A.P. (1988). Female choice selects for male sexual tail ornaments in the monogamous swallow. *Nature, 332*, 640–642.

Møller, A.P. (1990). Effects of a haematophagous mite on the barn swallow (*Hirundo rustica*): A test of the Hamilton and Zuk hypothesis. *Evolution, 44,* 771–784.

Møller, A.P. (1992). Female swallow preference for symmetric male sexual ornaments. *Nature, 357,* 238–240.

Møller, A.P., & Pomiankowski, A. (1993). Fluctuating asymmetry and sexual selection. *Genetica, 89,* 267–279.

Morton, J., & Johnson, M. (1989). Four ways for faces to be special. In A.W. Young & H.D. Ellis (Eds.), *Handbook of research on face processing* (pp.49–56). Amsterdam; North-Holland.

Morton, J., & Johnson, M.H. (1991). CONSPEC and CONLERN: A two-process theory of infant face recognition. *Psychological Review, 98,* 164–181.

Murphy, G.L., & Medin, D.L. (1985). The role of theories in conceptual coherence. *Psychological Review, 92,* 289–316.

Neumann, P.G. (1974). An attribute frequency model for the abstraction of prototypes. *Memory & Cognition, 2,* 241–248.

Nosofsky, R.M. (1988). Exemplar-based accounts of relations between classification, recognition and typicality. *Journal of Experimental Psychology: Learning, Memory & Cognition, 14,* 700–708.

O'Donald, P. (1977). Theoretical aspects of sexual selection. *Theoretical and Population Biology, 12,* 298–334.

Oldfield, R.C. (1954). Memory mechanisms and the theory of schemata. *British Journal of Psychology, 45,* 14–23.

Oldfield, R.C., & Zangwill, O.L. (1942). Head's conception of the schema and its application in contemporary British Psychology. Part I. Head's concept of the schema. *British Journal of Psychology, 32,* 267–286.

Oldfield, R.C., & Zangwill, O.L. (1943). Head's conception of the schema and its application in contemporary British Psychology. Part II. Critical analysis of head's theory. *British Journal of Psychology, 33,* 55–64.

O'Toole, A.J., Abdi, H., Deffenbacher, K.A., & Valentin, D. (1995). A perceptual learning theory of the information in faces. In T. Valentine (Ed.), *Cognitive and computational aspects of face recognition: Explorations in face space* (pp.159–182). London & New York: Routledge.

Osborne, E. (1970). *The Oxford companion to art.* Oxford: Clarendon Press.

Pagel, M. (1993). The design of animal signals. *Nature, 361,* 18–20.

Palmer, A.R., & Strobeck, C.A. (1986). Fluctuating asymmetry: measurement, analysis, pattern. *Annual Review of Ecology and Systematics, 17,* 391–421.

Palmer, S.E. (1975). Visual perception and world knowledge: Notes on a model of sensory–cognition interaction. In D.A. Norman, D.E. Rumelhart, & LNR Research Group, (Eds.), *Explorations in cognition.* San Francisco: W.H. Freeman.

Parsons, P.A. (1990). Fluctuating asymmetry: An epigenetic measure of stress. *Biological Review, 65,* 131–145.

Perkins, D. (1975). A definition of caricature and caricature and recognition. *Studies in the Anthropology of Visual Communication, 2,* 1–24.

Perrett, D.I., May, K.A., & Yoshikawa, S. (1994). Facial shape and judgements of female attractiveness. *Nature, 368,* 239–242.

Petrie, M. (1994). Improved growth and survival of offspring of peacocks with more elaborate trains. *Nature, 371,* 598–599.

Petrie, M., Halliday, T., & Sanders, C. (1991). Peahens prefer peacocks with elaborate trains. *Animal Behaviour, 41,* 323–331.

Pittenger, J.B. (1991). On the difficulty of averaging faces: Comments on Langlois and Roggman. *Psychological Science, 2,* 351–353.

Pomiankowski, A. (1994). Swordplay and sensory bias. *Nature, 368,* 494–495.

Pomiankowski, A., & Sheridan, L. (1994). Linked sexiness and choosiness. *Trends in Ecology & Evolution, 9,* 242–244.

Posner, M.I., & Keele, S.W. (1968). On the genesis of abstract ideas. *Journal of Experimental Psychology, 77,* 353–363.

Posner, M.I., & Keele, S.W. (1970). Retention of abstract ideas. *Journal of Experimental Psychology, 83,* 304–308.

Proctor, H.C. (1991). Courtship in the water mite *Neumania papillator*: Males capitalize on female adaptations for predation. *Animal Behaviour, 42,* 589–598.

Proctor, H.C. (1993). Sensory exploitation and the evolution of mating behaviour: a cladistic test using water mites (Acari: *Parasitengona*). *Animal Behaviour, 44,* 745–752.

Purtle, R.B. (1973). Peak shift: A review. *Psychological Bulletin, 80,* 408–421.

Ramus, C.F. (Ed.). (1978). *Daumier—120 great lithographs.* New York: Dover.

Reed, S.K. (1972). Pattern recognition and categorization. *Cognitive Psychology, 3,* 382–407.

Reed, S.K. (1973). *Psychological processes in pattern recognition.* New York: Academic Press.

Rhodes, G. (1985). *Mental representations of faces.* Unpublished doctoral dissertation, Stanford University, Stanford, CA, U.S.A.

Rhodes, G. (1988). Looking at faces: First-order and second-order features as determinants of facial appearance. *Perception, 17,* 43–63.

Rhodes, G. (1993). When do caricatures look good? *New Zealand Journal of Psychology, 22,* 113–116.

Rhodes, G., (1994). Secrets of the face. *New Zealand Journal of Psychology, 23,* 3–17.

Rhodes, G. (1996). The modularity of face recognition. In A. Kent, J.G. Williams, & C.M. Hall (Eds.), *Encyclopedia of Computer Science & Technology* (pp.261–280). New York: Marcel Dekker Inc.

Rhodes, G., Brake, S., & Atkinson, A. (1993). What's lost in inverted faces? *Cognition, 47,* 25–57.

Rhodes, G., Brennan, S., & Carey, S. (1987). Identification and ratings of caricatures: Implications for mental representations of faces. *Cognitive Psychology, 19,* 473–497.

Rhodes, G., Byatt, G., Tremewan, T., & Kennedy, A. (1996). Facial distinctiveness and the power of caricatures. Submitted for publication

Rhodes, G., Carey, S., Byatt, G., & Proffitt, F. (1996). [Recognition of caricatures, anticaricatures and lateral caricatures of famous faces]. Unpublished raw data.

Rhodes, G., & McLean, I.G. (1990). Distinctiveness and expertise effects with homogeneous stimuli: Towards a model of configural coding. *Perception, 19,* 773–794.

Rhodes, G., & Moody, J. (1990). Memory representations of unfamiliar faces: Coding of distinctive information. *New Zealand Journal of Psychology, 19,* 70–78.

Rhodes, G., & Proffitt, F., Grady, J., & Sumich, A.L. (In preparation). Facial symmetry and the biology of beauty.

Rhodes, G., Tan, S., Brake, S., & Taylor, K. (1989). Expertise and configural coding in face recognition. *British Journal of Psychology, 80,* 313–331.

Rhodes, G., & Tremewan, T. (1994). Understanding face recognition: Caricature effects, inversion and the homogeneity problem. *Visual Cognition, 1,* 275–311.

Rhodes, G., & Tremewan, T. (1996). Averageness, exaggeration and facial attractiveness. *Psychological Science, 7,* 105–110.

Ridley, M. (1992). Research news—Swallows and scorpionflies find symmetry beautiful. *Science, 257,* 327–328.

Ridley. M. (1993). *The red queen: Sex and the evolution of human nature.* Harmondsworth, UK: Penguin Books Ltd.

Rock, I., & Di Vita, J. (1987). A case of viewer-centered object perception. *Cognitive Psychology, 19,* 280–293.

Rosch, E.H. (1973a). On the internal structure of perceptual and semantic categories. In T.E. Moore (Ed.), *Cognitive development and the acquisition of language* (pp.111–144). New York: Academic Press.

Rosch, E.H. (1973b). Natural categories. *Cognitive Psychology, 4,* 328–350.

Rosch, E.H. (1973c). Cognitive reference points. *Cognitive Psychology, 7,* 532–547.

Rosch, E.H. (1975). The nature of mental codes for color categories. *Journal of Experimental Psychology: General, 104,* 192–233.

Rosch, E.H. (1978). Principles of categorisation. In E. Rosch & B.B. Lloyd (Eds.), *Cognition and categorisation* (pp.27–48). Hillsdale, NJ: Lawrence Erlbaum Associates Inc.

Rosch, E., Mervis, C.B., Gray, W.D., Johnson, D.M., & Boyes-Braem, P. (1976). Basic objects in natural categories. *Cognitive Psychology, 8,* 382–439.

Rosch, E.H., Simpson, C., & Miller, R.S. (1976). Structural bases of typicality effects. *Journal of Experimental Psychology: Human Perception & Performance, 2,* 491–502.

Roth, I., & Bruce, V. (1995). *Perception and representation: Current issues* (2nd ed.). Buckingham, UK: Open University Press.

Rowland, W.J. (1989a). Mate choice and the supernormality effect in female sticklebacks (*Gasterosteus aculeatus*). *Behavioral Ecology & Sociobiology, 24,* 433–438.

Rowland, W.J. (1989b). The ethological basis of mate choice in male sticklebacks, *Gasterosteus aculeatus. Animal Behaviour, 38,* 112–120.

Rumelhart, D.E., McClelland, J.L., & the PDP Research Group. (1986). *Parallel distributed processing: Explorations in the microstructure of cognition, Volume 2: Psychological and Biological Models.* Cambridge, MA: MIT Press, A Bradford Book.

Ryan, M.J. (1983). Sexual selection and communication in a neotropical frog, *Physalaemus pustulosus. Evolution, 37,* 261–272.

Ryan, M.J. (1990). Sexual selection, sensory systems and sensory exploitation. In D. Futuyma & J. Antonovics (Eds.), *Oxford Surveys in Evolutionary Biology, 7,* 157–195.

Ryan, M.J., Fox, J.H., Wilczynski, W., & Rand, A.S. (1990). Sexual selection for sensory exploitation in the frog *Physalaemus pustulosus. Nature, 343,* 66–67.

Ryan, M.J., & Keddy-Hector, A. (1992). Directional patterns of female mate choice and the role of sensory biases. *American Naturalist, 139,* S4–S35.

Ryan, M.J., & Rand, A.S. (1990). The sensory basis of sexual selection for complex calls in the Tungara frog, *Physalaemus pustulosus* (sexual selection for sensory exploitation). *Evolution, 44,* 305–314.

Ryan, M.J., & Rand, A.S. (1993). Sexual selection and signal evolution: The ghost of biases past. *Philosophical Transactions of the Royal Society of London, Series B, 340,* 187–195.

Ryan, T.A., & Schwartz, C. B. (1956). Speed of perception as a function of mode of presentation. *American Journal of Psychology, 69*, 60–69.

Searcy, J.H., & Bartlett, J.C. (1996). Inversion and processing of component and spatial-relational information in faces. *Journal of Experimental Psychology: Human Perception & Performance, 22*, 904–915.

Searcy, W.A. (1992). Song repertoire and mate choice in birds. *American Zoologist, 32*, 71–80.

Sekuler, R., & Blake, R. (1990). *Perception* (2nd ed.). New York: McGraw-Hill.

Sergent, J. (1984a). An investigation into component and configural processes underlying face perception. *British Journal of Psychology, 75*, 221–242.

Sergent, J. (1984b). Configural processing of faces in the left and right cerebral hemispheres. *Journal of Experimental Psychology: Human Perception & Performance, 10*, 554–572.

Shanks, D.R. (1991a). Categorization by a connectionist network. *Journal of Experimental Psychology: Learning, Memory & Cognition, 17*, 433–443.

Shanks, D.R. (1991b). Some parallels between associative learning and object classification. In J.-A Meyer & S. Wilson (Eds.), *From animals to animals* (pp. 337–343). Cambridge, MA: MIT Press.

Shaw, K. (1995). Phylogenetic tests of the sensory exploitation model of sexual selection. *Trends in Ecology & Evolution, 10*, 117–120.

Shepard, R.N. (1990). *Mind sights*. New York: W.H. Freeman & Co.

Shepherd, J.W., Davies, G.M., & Ellis, H.D. (1981). Studies of cue saliency. In G. Davies, H. Ellis, & J. Shepherd (Eds.), *Perceiving and remembering faces*. London: Academic Press.

Simmons, L.W. (1987). Female choice contributes to offspring fitness in the field cricket, *Gryllus bimaculatus* (De Geer). *Behavioral Ecology & Sociobiology, 21*, 313–321.

Small, M.F. (1992). Female choice in mating. *American Scientist, 80*, 142–151.

Smith, E.E., & Medin, D.L. (1981). *Categories and concepts*. Cambridge, MA: Harvard University Press.

Smith, H.G., & Montgomerie, R. (1991). Sexual selection and the tail ornaments of North American barn swallows. *Behavioral Ecology & Sociobiology, 28*, 195–201.

Solso, R.L. (1991). *Cognitive psychology* (3rd ed.). Boston: Allyn & Bacon.

Solso, R.L., & McCarthy, J.E. (1981a). Prototype formation of faces: A case of pseudomemory. *British Journal of Psychology, 72*, 499–503.

Solso, R.L., & McCarthy, J.E. (1981b). Prototype formation: Central tendency model vs. attribute frequency model. *Bulletin of the Psychonomic Society, 17*, 10–11.

Solso, R.L., & Raynis, S.A. (1979). Prototype formation from imaged, kinesthetically, and visually presented geometric figures. *Journal of Experimental Psychology: Human Perception & Performance, 5*, 701–712.

Spence, K.W. (1937). The differential response in animals to stimuli varying within a single dimension. *Psychological Review, 44*, 430–444.

Staddon, J.E.R. (1975). A note on the evolutionary significance of "supernormal" stimuli. *American Naturalist, 109*, 541–545.

Sternglantz, S.H, Gray, J.L., & Murakami, M. (1977). Adult preferences for infantile facial features: An ethological approach. *Animal Behavior, 25*, 108–115.

Stevenage, S.V. (1995a). Can caricatures really produce distinctiveness effects? *British Journal of Psychology, 86*, 127–146.

Stevenage, S.V. (1995b). Demonstration of a caricature advantage in children. *Cahiers de Psychologie Cognitive, 14*, 325–341.

Strauss, M.S. (1979). Abstraction of prototypical information by adults and 10-month-old infants. *Journal of Experimental Psychology: Human Learning & Memory, 5*, 618–632.

Suboski, M.D. (1990). Releaser-induced recognition learning. *Psychological Review, 97*, 271–284.

Sullivan, B.K. (1983). Sexual selection in Woodhouse's toad (*Bufo woodhousei*). II. Female choice. *Animal Behaviour, 31*, 1011–1017.

Swaddle, J.P., & Cuthill, I.C. (1995). Asymmetry and human facial attractiveness: Symmetry may not always be beautiful. *Proceedings of the Royal Society of London, B, 261*, 111–116.

Takane, Y., & Sergent, J. (1983). Multidimensional models for reaction times and same–different judgments. *Psychometrika, 48*, 393–423.

Takano, Y. (1989). Perception of rotated forms: A theory of information types. *Cognitive Psychology, 21*, 1–59.

Tanaka, J.W. (1990). Caricature recognition in a neural network. *Proceedings of the XII Annual Conference of the Cognitive Science Society* (pp. 622–628). Hillsdale, NJ: Lawrence Erlbaum Associates Inc.

Tanaka, J. W., & Farah, M. J. (1993). Parts and wholes in face recognition. *Quarterly Journal of Experimental Psychology, 46A*, 225–245.

Tanaka, J.W., & Simon, V.G. (1996). Caricature recognition in a neural network. *Visual Cognition*, in press.

Tarr, M.J., & Bülthoff, H.H. (1995). Is human object recognition better described by geon structure descriptions or by multiple views? Comment on Biederman and Gerhardstein (1993). *Journal of Experimental Psychology: Human Perception & Performance, 21*, 1494–1505.

Tarr, M.J., & Chawarski, M. (1993). *The concurrent coding of object-based and view-based representations*. Paper presented at the 34th annual meeting of the Psychonomic Society, Washington, DC.

Tarr, M.J., Hayward, W.G., Gauthier, I., & Williams, P. (1994). *Geon recognition is viewpoint dependent*. Paper presented at the 35th annual meeting of the Psychonomic Society, St Louis, MO.

Tarr, M.J., & Pinker, S. (1989). Mental rotation and orientation-dependence in shape recognition. *Cognitive Psychology, 21*, 233–282.

Tarr, M.J., & Pinker, S. (1990). When does human object recognition use a viewer-centered reference frame? *Psychological Science, 1*, 253–256.

ten Cate, C., & Bateson, P. (1988). Sexual selection: The evolution of conspicuous characteristics in birds by means of imprinting. *Evolution, 42*, 1355–1358.

Terrace, H.S. (1966). Stimulus control. In W.K. Honig (Ed.), *Operant behavior: Areas of research & application*. New York: Appleton-Century-Crofts.

Terrace, H.S. (1968). Discrimination learning, the peak shift, and behavioral contrast. *Journal of Experimental Analysis of Behavior, 11*, 727–741.

Thomas, D.R. (1993). A model for adaptation-level effects on stimulus generalization. *Psychological Review, 100*, 658–673.

Thomas, D.R., Mood, K., Morrison, S., & Wiertelak, E. (1991). Peak shift revisited: A test of alternative interpretations. *Journal of Experimental Psychology: Animal Behavior Processes, 17*, 130–140.

Thornhill, R. (1992). Female preference for the pheromone of males with low fluctuating asymmetry in the Japanese scorpionfly (*Panorpa japonica*: Mecoptera). *Behavioral Ecology, 3*, 277–283.

Thornhill, R. & Gangestad, S.W. (1994). Human fluctuating asymmetry and sexual behavior. *Psychological Science, 5*, 297–302.

Tinbergen, N. (1951). *The study of instinct.* New York: Oxford University Press.

Tinbergen, N. (1953). *The herring gull's world: A study of the social behavior of birds.* London: Collins.

Trivers, R.L. (1972). Parental investment and sexual selection. In B. Campbell (Ed.), *Sexual selection and the descent of man* (pp.136–179). London: Heinemann.

Turk, M., & Pentland, A. (1991). Eigenfaces for recognition. *Journal of Cognitive Neuroscience, 3*, 71–86.

Tversky, B.T., & Baratz, D. (1985). Memory for faces: Are caricatures better than photographs? *Memory & Cognition, 13*, 45–49.

Tversky, B.T., & Hemenway, K. (1984). Objects, parts and categories. *Journal of Experimental Psychology: General, 113*, 169–193.

Tyrrell, D.J., Anderson, J.T., Clubb, M., & Bradbury, A. (1987). Infant recognition of the correspondence between photographs and caricatures of human faces. *Bulletin of the Psychonomic Society, 25*, 41–43.

Ullman, S. (1989). Aligning pictorial descriptions: An approach to object recognition. *Cognition, 32*, 193–254.

Valentine, T. (1988). Upside-down faces : A review of the effect of inversion upon face recognition. *British Journal of Psychology, 79*, 471–491.

Valentine, T. (1991). A unified account of the effects of distinctiveness, inversion, and race in face recognition. *Quarterly Journal of Experimental Psychology, 43A*, 161–204.

Valentine, T., & Bruce, V. (1986a). Recognizing familiar faces: The role of distinctiveness and familiarity. *Canadian Journal of Psychology, 40*, 300–305.

Valentine, T., & Bruce, V. (1986b). The effects of distinctiveness in recognising and classifying faces. *Perception, 15*, 525–535.

Valentine, T., & Bruce, V. (1986c). The effect of race, inversion and encoding activity upon face recognition. *Acta Psychologica, 61*, 259–273.

Valentine, T., & Endo, M. (1992). Towards an exemplar model of face processing: The effects of race and distinctiveness. *Quarterly Journal of Experimental Psychology, 44A*, 671–703.

Vokey, J.R., & Read, J.D. (1992). Familiarity, memorability, and the effect of typicality on the recognition of faces. *Memory & Cognition, 20*, 291–302.

Wallace, A.R. (1889). *Darwinism.* Macmillan: London.

Wallace, A.R. (1891). *Natural selection and tropical nature: Essays on descriptive and theoretical biology.* Macmillan: London.

Walton, G.E., & Bower, T.G.R. (1993). Newborns form "prototypes" in less than 1 minute. *Psychological Science, 4*, 203–205.

Watson, P.W., & Thornhill, R. (1994). Fluctuating asymmetry and sexual selection. *Trends in Ecology & Evolution, 9*, 21–25.

Weary, D.M., Guilford, T.C., & Weisman, R.G. (1993). A product of discriminative learning may lead to female preferences for elaborate males. *Evolution, 47*, 336–340.

Wechsler, J. (1982). *A human comedy: Physiognomy and caricature in 19th century Paris.* Chicago: University of Chicago Press.

Wedekind, C. (1992). Detailed information about parasites revealed by sexual ornamentation. *Proceedings of the Royal Society of London, Series B, 247*, 169–174.

Weiss, S.J., & Weissman, R.D. (1992). Generalization peak shift for autoshaped and operant key pecks. *Journal of the Experimental Analysis of Behavior, 57,* 127–143.

Westwood, H.R. (1932). *Modern caricaturists.* London: Lovat Dickson Ltd.

Wilding, J., & Valentine, E. (1985). One man's memory for prose, faces and names. *British Journal of Psychology, 76,* 215–219.

Winograd, E. (1981). Elaboration and distinctiveness in memory for faces. *Journal of Experimental Psychology: Human Learning & Memory, 7,* 181–190.

Woodworth, R.S. (1938). *Experimental psychology.* London: Methuen.

Yin, R.K. (1969). Looking at upside-down faces. *Journal of Experimental Psychology, 81,* 141–145.

Yin, R.K. (1970). Face recognition: A dissociable ability? *Neuropsychologia, 8,* 395–402.

Young, A.W., Hay, D.C., McWeeny, K.H., Flude, B.M., & Ellis, A.W. (1985). Matching familiar and unfamiliar faces on internal and external features. *Perception, 14,* 737–746.

Young, A.W., Hellawell, D., & Hay, D.C. (1987). Configurational information in face perception. *Perception, 16,* 747–759.

Zahavi, A. (1975). Mate selection—a selection for a handicap. *Journal of Theoretical Biology, 53,* 205–214.

Zahavi, A. (1991). On the definition of sexual selection, Fisher's model, and the evolution of waste and of signals in general. *Animal Behaviour, 42,* 501–503.

Zebrowitz, L.A. (in press). *Reading faces.* Boulder, CO: Westview Press.

Author index

Subject index